A. J. CONYERS

E CLIPSE
THE

H EAVEN
OF

Rediscovering the Hope of a World Beyond

INTERVARSITY PRESS
DOWNERS GROVE, ILLINOIS 60515

InterVarsity Press is the book-publishing division of InterVarsity Christian Fellowship, a student movement active on campus at hundreds of universities, colleges and schools of nursing in the United States of America, and a member movement of the International Fellowship of Evangelical Students. For information about local and regional activities, write Public Relations Dept., InterVarsity Christian Fellowship, 6400 Schroeder Rd., P.O. Box 7895, Madison, WI 53707-7895.

All Scripture quotations, unless otherwise indicated, are taken from the HOLY BIBLE, NEW INTERNATIONAL VERSION. Copyright © 1973, 1978, 1984 International Bible Society. Used by permission of Zondervan Publishing House. All rights reserved.

Cover illustration: Jerry Tiritilli

ISBN 0-8308-1389-6

Printed in the United States of America

Library of Congress Cataloging-in-Publication Data

Conyers, A. J., 1944-
    The eclipse of heaven: rediscovering the hope of a world beyond/
  A. J. Conyers.
      p.   cm.
    Includes bibliographical references.
    ISBN 0-8308-1389-6
    1. Heaven—Christianity.   2. Transcendence of God.
  3. Christianity and religious humanism.   I. Title.
  BT846.2.C66 1992
  236'.24—dc20   92-21094
                                     CIP

17	16	15	14	13	12	11	10	9	8	7	6	5	4	3	2	1
05	04	03	02	01	00	99	98	97	96	95	94	93	92			

Dedicated to the memory of
Jim Leathers
(1942-1991)
Who lived with boldness
because he lived
with heaven in his heart

Acknowledgments

I wish to express my gratitude to all those who have contributed to the completion of this book, including my editor at InterVarsity Press, Rodney Clapp; the academic secretary for the Charleston Southern University religion department, Barbara Parker; and my entire family—who both supported this project with prayer and offered many helpful comments. Also, I would add to this list Mrs. Margaret Gilmore, Dr. Scott Walker and Reverend Frank Martick. All of these, out of generous hearts and providing much wisdom, helped me believe that these issues should come to the attention of a world hungering for a rumor of heaven.

Acknowledgments

CHAPTER 1

THE ECLIPSE
OF HEAVEN

Eclipse of the light of heaven,
eclipse of God—such indeed is the character
of the historic hour through which
the world is passing.

Martin Buber

• • •

WE LIVE IN A WORLD NO LONGER UNDER HEAVEN. AT LEAST IN MOST PEOPLE'S
minds and imaginations that vision of reality has become little more
than a caricature, conjuring up the saints and angels of baroque frescoes.
And in the church only a hint remains of the power it once exercised
in the hearts of believers.

It's true that most Americans, when responding to George Gallup's
polls, say they believe in heaven; and similar results are found in European studies.[1] But the problem with taking polls to determine who believes in heaven is that when the respondents answer,"Yes, of course,
I believe in heaven," they are only engaging in easy speculation. They
give answer to a life-and-death question when nothing really important
is at stake. It's only an opinion given at leisure.

I learned that it's a different matter when people—especially large numbers of people—are caught up in a general crisis. When that happens, people resort to what they may not otherwise even recognize as their most reliable beliefs. Thus, inevitably, they reveal their fundamental values.

Cataclysm and Cosmology

A few years ago Hurricane Hugo slammed into the coast of South Carolina at Charleston. What immediately strikes you about a natural disaster is that it has the power to upset your sense of the permanence and reliability of the physical world. We translate the Greek word *kosmos* as *world*. Yet the early use of the word implied much more than the physical, sensible world: it implied order and wholeness. Hurricanes disrupt one's sense of kosmos. The idea of kosmos is really a sentiment about reliability—and a natural disaster undermines that sentiment; order is replaced by chaos, and certainty is replaced by questions.

Many of my neighbors found that the trees once standing so harmlessly and all in order outside their front doors suddenly came thundering into their living rooms and attics. Others, nearer the coast, found the beauty of the Atlantic Ocean turning ugly and life-threatening, washing the treasures of a lifetime in houses, furniture and boats, out to sea. The kosmos was disrupted, and questions were in order. But what kind of questions were we asking? And how are the questions we ask today different from those of a generation that might have held to a stronger vision of a transcendent reality? Down through history, other natural disasters have raised important questions about human existence. A prominent example would be the Lisbon earthquake of 1755, which claimed some ten to fifteen thousand lives and reduced three-quarters of the city to rubble.[2] Today that quake is remembered primarily for the fact that it resulted in vast social and intellectual disturbance, bringing profound changes to settled European habits of thought. It also began a period of the most extraordinary moral and theological reflection. Urgent questions were brought to the surface in public life. The world, it became apparent, was less stable than Europeans had been accustomed to thinking. What was disturbed, of course, was the physical world; but what came into question was the whole order of the world, a world that was preserved under the power of heaven. Both the age of revolution in France and Germany and the age of Wesleyan revival in England are often associated with the catastrophic events in Portugal.

Over a period of time, three lines of questioning emerged. Even a brief account of these conveys the fact of this period's intense desire to deal with fundamental issues:

1. How does the earthquake speak (or does it) of divine providence?

A widespread sentiment took root that this catastrophe was a divine judgment against a sinful city. With such a dreadful judgment, the offense must necessarily have been equally dreadful, an impression made all the stronger since at the time of the first shocks, on All Saints Day, the churches of Lisbon were crowded with worshipers. A famous Jesuit speaker, Malagrida, was a typical example of an extreme point of view:

> Learn, O Lisbon, that the destroyers of our houses, palaces, churches, and convents, the cause of the death of so many people and of the flames that devoured such vast treasures, are your abominable sins.[3]

Others, interestingly, thought of the earthquake as judgment upon the Jesuits, who were found in great numbers in Lisbon. Still others, notably in England and Germany, made the earthquake a case against Catholicism. But, for the most part, both theologians and the general populace of Europe refrained from this extremity of moral judgment against a whole population, even though those "earthquake sermons" were common fare for years to come.

Some, while seeing God as directly and intentionally responsible for the earthquake, attempted to defend him from the harsh picture of divine judgment the moral extremists had painted. A Franciscan preacher argued that the quake was a form of divine mercy. After all, he maintained, Portugal deserved much worse: God could have justifiably engulfed the whole nation, or at the least, destroyed the entire city of Lisbon. In view of what he *could* have done, God had performed only enough to warn Lisbon—and indeed the world—of his just displeasure. His action—however alarming it was at the time—was an act of mercy![4]

At the other end of the scale of possible eighteenth-century arguments was the view that the earthquake could only be seen as a natural disaster.

A Spanish Benedictine monk who inclined toward a more scientific explanation was impressed by the fact that one of the recent earthquakes had been felt in two cities, Oviedo and Cádiz, at precisely the same time; and the cities were 500 miles apart. Obviously there was some deeper phenomenon that affects the earth's surface at two such distant places at once. He attributed the result to the latest matter of scientific excitement, electricity. This Benedictine thinker saw the catastrophe as one of a whole range of fatal events that are explained purely by natural causes. The point, he insisted, is that one must be ready for death at any time: it is not, as others tried to say, a special sign that one could use to read God's will into history.

2. The second question to arise out of the rubble of the Lisbon earthquake concerned the stability of social institutions. Perhaps nothing could really be depended on for long, and therefore time-honored social conventions and traditions were not reliable guides. Fixed orders and fixed purposes become impossible when nothing—including the ground under one's feet—can be depended upon.

For those of us who grew up in the United States, which found its national beginnings during this time, it is hard to imagine that much of Europe was affected by a profound historical pessimism. The earthquake had seemed a crowning event in a whole series of disasters. The Turks had appeared on the doorsteps of Europe on three occasions in the eighteenth century. The Seven Years' War had ravaged the continent and wasted human life as well as economic resources. The new colonial possibilities in the New World had driven much of Europe mad with greed for enormous profits. Slave trade was expanding at a time when conscience had almost ruled it out in the home nations. There were attempts at assassination—of Louis XV in 1757 and of José of Portugal in 1758. A French poet of the eighteenth century, Le Brun, called his age the "infamous and atrocious century," in a poem on the great calamity of that time. The poem's title was "Ode to the Sun on the Misfortunes of the Earth since the Lisbon Earthquake of 1755." "Perish the memory," he said, "of our lamentable days."[5]

3. The third question to arise prominently regarded the relationship between human mortality and moral responsibility.

The young philosopher Immanuel Kant was to see this aspect of the earthquake's effect as the only profitable one. No one could penetrate the purposes of God. Nor could anyone conclude that the world, in and of itself, reveals any stability of purpose. In spite of this fact, or perhaps because of it, we realize in the face of such a disaster that we are not created for this life only. There is a greater reality, and therefore a greater obligation, that impresses itself upon our hearts. Disasters only remind us that "if in this life only we have hope, we are of all men most miserable." It is the transcendence implied by moral duty that answers the fragmented and incomplete world of death and disasters.

The remarkable character of all three of these lines of questions, however, does not depend upon the actual answers that were given. It is in the questions themselves that we, in our age, should find something distinct, something different from our own time. We have moved too far away from the world of the Lisbon earthquake to have a wholly reliable understanding of what the Europeans of that day felt. But generally what we find is that these questions arose in an atmosphere that was still affected by the "bright shadow of heaven." Whether the answers are naturalistic—as in the answer of that Benedictine scientist—or whether it solved the riddle in terms of divine wrath, or whether it sought to define the source of stability in the world, the question at least was of the world and its relation to a transcendent reality. There was still the vivid sense that things must be seen, worked out, and understood in reference to heaven.

Now let's return to Hugo. While this hurricane was nothing like the Lisbon earthquake in terms of lost lives or of its psychological impact upon a whole continent (which is the lasting legacy of the 1755 quake), it was nevertheless a true disaster. The meaning of a *disaster* is carried in the word itself, which originally implied being "separated from the stars." In a disaster, people lose their orientation, the world loses its usual appearance, it breaks apart, and it is no longer clear how things are to fit together again. By that standard—along with the loss of life and property—we in this region of the Carolinas experienced a disturbance of the stars, a disorientation.

After the storm had passed we were without electrical power for some time, as long as a month in some communities. My own neighborhood was fortunate; in eight days we had the lights on again.

In the meantime, I spent the daylight hours clearing the wilderness of blown-down trees and the debris, joining with neighbors in their efforts to salvage some order from the general destruction.

At night, for the most part, I took stock of the outside world. Reading by candlelight and listening to my battery-powered radio, I learned bit by bit the story of the larger disaster. A few miles away, in McClellanville and Awendaw, people's houses and belongings had been scattered to the winds. On Sullivan's Island some homes had been left uninhabitable. Others had been washed completely away, into the marsh; in some cases nothing was left where the house had stood but a littered patch of sand. Experts had warned for years that these barrier islands were no place to build homes. Now nature had reinforced the lesson with a vengeance.

I suspect some features of the Lisbon experience were repeated even on this occasion. It might be difficult, for instance, for a preacher to resist the temptation to preach about the one who "builds his house upon the sand." But, in fact, although we still have not had adequate time to reflect on these events, and although the "religious" note is never entirely missing, especially in such circumstances, I wonder now if there is not a decided peculiarity in our response—in the response of late twentieth-century people.

I noted on one occasion—only one—that a radio commentator said,

"Wait till this Sunday! In spite of all the inconveniences, and in spite of the devastated church buildings, there will be more people in church this Sunday than at almost any time you and I have known."

The statement seemed, at the time, a bit intemperate: just a trifle grandiose and, in the sentiment it expressed, not quite believable. But then, public figures were saying many things in those days after Hugo, aiming more to build morale than to provide us with a disinterested analysis. That is understandable, and even proper under the circumstances. So far as I know, however, that was the only time an optimistic comment of that sort concerning the religious life of the community was aired over the public media. The religious community was certainly visible, and involved, but as far as any general anticipation of a changed spiritual climate, or of a renewal of faith, this incautious prediction of full churches was the only time I noticed that kind of expectation expressed. And this was the case even though there was a continued effort, not only to keep people informed, but to keep the spirits high.

I went to church that Sunday. We sat in the darkened sanctuary, without sound system or air conditioning, and with the buzzing of our neighbors' chain saws in the background, we worshiped. I did not do a scientific survey of churches, but for that particular church there was a small crowd in attendance that day, not a large one. Moreover, they were almost all "regulars," those who would be there even under adverse conditions, and they were not at all ushered out of their houses and into church by the fearsome aspect of the recent display of nature's powers. And, from what I learned, the experience was roughly the same in all of the area churches.

Nevertheless, I noticed something else over the next few days, as I listened to radio, keeping in touch with the world. At least half a dozen times a day the broadcast featured a local psychologist or psychiatrist. Typically the psychologist told us we were experiencing a kind of grief; but that was O.K.—it's normal. We also heard about certain stages of adjustment through grief: denial, anger, depression, and (it was hoped) acceptance.

What had the great catastrophe brought us? An awareness of the power of God over creation? Or of the frailty of the human condition? Or of the incompatibility of human longing with the narrowness of mortal existence? Or was it only that our psyche was out of kilter and needed fixing? Judging by media attention, by far the most urgently important topic seemed to be how we *felt*.

Literally hours of interviews were devoted to how people were "coping" emotionally, or whether they were emerging from the shock of the storm and becoming "optimistic" again. It has for a long time, of course, been an intense interest of the media to take soundings of the public's subjective response to whatever is happening. (The PBS news broadcast this morning began, "What is the *mood* of the American people now that the war has taken a new turn?") The media seem to be responding to a conviction that there is something important to be discovered when we "get in touch with ourselves."

To a remarkable extent it seemed that we were focusing not on what had happened to the world around us, but on what was happening inside us. The most urgent question was not what all of this might mean, but how we had each experienced it. Naturally people were still interested in the objective facts of the hurricane and its aftermath; but to the extent that any intellectual response took place it was seldom in terms of questions about the *kosmos* (the nature of the world), much less *Theos* (or questions about God). Instead there was an intense focus on *psyche*— on personal experience.

I became aware then, more than ever, of how our world views these matters in its own peculiar fashion. When even in the extremities of natural disaster we no longer ask how this illuminates the mystery "over us," but instead attend to the enigma "within us," then a gigantic shift has taken place in our picture of the world. The light of heaven has dimmed for us, and we look within for a light to mark the path.

Thinking in Isolation: A Modern Perspective
In this shift of focus we are presented with a series of questions. First,

does it really matter how we relate to the world outside of us? Second, if so, are we at all limited by that world, subject to it—that is, subject to a reality that transcends our own knowledge and experience? Further, third, do we conceive of that world as itself subject to a Will and a Reality that sets the very boundary and purpose of that world?

If I answer "yes" to all three of these, then I am saying (1) yes, I am related to the world, (2) that world is more than I can comprehend, and (3) both that world and I are comprehended by a greater reality that is "over us." In that case, it becomes very clear to me that the centrally important thing to understand and to set right has to do with relationship. It can be seen that, in this case, the idea of heaven, of a comprehending and transcending reality, is vitally important. It answers the question whether this great, incomprehensible reality is one that I *can* relate to; or whether it is, in the final analysis, chaotic, purposeless, and impersonal, or else indifferent with regard to my life.

On the other hand, if my response to the world takes place almost altogether on the level of "my will," or "my feelings," or "my intellect," then no question of relationship comes up. And the question of "right relationship" can appear, if not irrelevant, at least not urgent.

The reality of heaven, in a world so confined to the boundaries of personal experience, is one that can hardly mean the same thing. It is interesting that when sociologist Andrew Greeley made a survey of attitudes toward heaven, he found that "most Americans expect a continuation of life on earth, but without the wars, diseases and other inconveniences that cramp their present pursuit of happiness."[6]

If the concept of heaven enters our minds at all it takes the form of life without limits. It seems to be that aspect of heaven that accords with the modern spirit. But a life without limits is a life without an "outside," or an "other." And a life without a strong sense of an "other" is a life without relationship—a life of freedom in its isolation, one made desolate, but unimpeded. What is the meaning, then, of this focus on inward adjustments, on "coping," regaining one's optimistic spirit? What is the great concern for working through a grief *process?* Is not grief about something that is lost, or is it only about itself?

I have before me a stenographer's pad I was using to write occasional notes during that period. Two days after the hurricane and in the midst of all the "coping" with its aftermath, I suppose I had heard enough of psychology over my battery-powered radio. In the notebook I wrote, "The storm may have stricken people with terror, for a brief few minutes, but not with awe. We think of life no longer as relating to a great unseen and outside power. The transcendent 'Thou' is missing from our experience of the world." I went on to describe what I was hearing from the realm of psychology: four or five stages of the grief process, followed by six steps to help you cope with "your grief, your anger, etc."

I must have been longing for an old-time prophet—even if he would fit awkwardly in our age—when I asked: "Would it not have been healthier, more realistic, more courageous, to say that what we have to deal with is not the equilibrium of a psyche that got tipped over, but a massive foreign, unknown, alien power? It knocked our plans and our houses into a cocked hat, and when it was done everything was turned around, not only inside us, but outside, actually! If it was not God, at least it was nature. And if it was not a manifestation of personal will in the universe, at least it paid not the least attention to our personal wills. This event had to do, not with the inside of us, but with the huge otherness of a world outside of us. It let us know, whether providentially or not, that reality includes something far greater than 'me,' and it is not an illusion, but a powerful reality with 135 miles per hour winds." The preachers of an earlier day did not forget the inside of experience, but they also did not forget the great outside.

"Nothing over Us"

Something P. T. Forsyth wrote in 1907 has proved to be hauntingly prophetic. It applies more to our time than to his when he said, "If within us we find nothing over us we succumb to what is around us."[7] Can anyone seriously doubt that our generation has almost entirely lost its capacity for what was once a very powerful sentiment: namely, that which transcends the world, that which is "over us"?

Of course, finding "nothing over us" means more than disbelieving in a doctrine of heaven. Whether one believes in heaven in a dogmatic sense is not the crisis I am referring to here, nor is it the cause of a crisis. But it may well be the symptom of a crisis. It may be the logical extension of thinking that resists any kind of transcendence, that insists upon finding its purpose and its happiness in this life and in no other. Moreover, this resistance to what was once an all-pervading sentiment—a belief that the pain and struggles of this life find their resolution in an order of being outside of time, in eternity—is a significant clue to the way our sorely troubled world tries to live.

It is not only heaven that we have half-forgotten, of course. The idea of hell, the final judgment, and the kingdom of God—and whatever these once meant to people—have fallen by the busy wayside of a world preoccupied by its ambitions and its fears for *this* life. The fact that we have almost dropped any transcendent orientation in life reveals something of the modern heart and mind. We may find it a more important gauge to the character of our time than any war, any revolution, any economic or political development. Even to one without religious commitment and theological convictions, it should be an unsettling thought that this world is attempting to chart its way through some of the most perilous waters in history, having now decided to ignore what was for nearly two millennia its fixed point of reference—its North Star. The certainty of judgment, the longing for heaven, the dread of hell: these are not prominent considerations in our modern discourse about the important matters of life. But they once were. Can we so easily assume that they served no purpose other than to mirror the superstitions or the powerlessness of medieval monks and frontier preachers? Of course, other peoples—millions of them, and generations of them—have also lived without any purpose higher than their own lives and their own possessions. In that, we are not unique. Our generation, however, has distinguished itself in that it has lived this way thinking we had no other choice—though a few even have done so out of conviction.

We have inoculated ourselves against that choice, as a matter of fact, by calling it "medieval" and by learning (though you and I, as a rule, would be hard-pressed to come up with a contemporary example) that a danger lies in becoming "so heavenly minded that we are no earthly good." We desire control, not submission; gain, not sacrifice. And as a result we call ourselves "pragmatists." Being down to earth means we value results. We were encouraged by Marxists to say that philosophers have told us many things about the world, but "the point is to change it." And we were told by the example of many capitalists that "the point is to use it." The pragmatism of either cannot be faulted. But *pragmatism* is simply another word for nontranscendent values.

Consequently, our ability to articulate the idea that life exists for something higher, something beyond itself, suffers. We speak of rewards in terms of this life only. This world, with its internal means and goals, must be self-sufficient and self-justifying. The resolute words of St. Paul in his first Corinthian letter—"If only for this life we have hope in Christ, we are to be pitied more than all men" (15:19)—reflect the radically transcendent values of the apostles and the early church. Whether these words are taken seriously by the contemporary church, especially in Western Europe and North America, should be a question of immense interest to every Christian. And whether the loss of that sentiment has not left a portentous vacuum in public life is a question of importance to every thinking person. So we are faced with inevitable questions: What happens to a world that has abandoned its hope for heaven and has substituted dreams and longings that lodge themselves in a world without heaven? What happens, in a word, when a strong transcendent purpose no longer operates upon human lives and human societies? What powers are invoked, and what is lost, when the highest goals of human existence must emerge from the possibilities within life?

A First Step

Our search for an answer must begin, however, with an awareness that it is not really the world that holds a vision of heaven. It is always the church that holds the vision *for* the world—and if the world is influenced by that vision, it is because the church has made it vivid and convincing.

So an initial question must be faced. How has the church fit into this general picture of the abandonment of heaven? It is to that vital question we turn next.

CHAPTER 2

THE CHURCH'S
FAILING VISION

The Christian reader, if he have had no
accounts of the city later than Bunyan's time,
will be surprised to hear that almost every
street has its church, and that the reverend
clergy are nowhere held in higher respect
than at Vanity Fair.

Nathaniel Hawthorne,
''The Celestial Railroad''

• • •

OCCASIONALLY, OVER THE COURSE OF YEARS, SOMEONE CALLS ATTENTION TO
the incredible gap between what the church says it believes and what
it actually proclaims with any passionate intensity. More than fifty years
ago, the famous Scottish theologian John Baillie wrote:

I will not ask how often during the last twenty-five years you and
I have listened to an old-style warning against the flames of hell. I
will not even ask how many sermons have been preached in our
hearing about a future day of reckoning when men shall reap according as they have sown. It will be enough to ask how many preachers,
during these years, have dwelt on the joys of the heavenly rest with
anything like the old ardent love and impatient longing, or have

spoken of the world that now is as a place of sojourn or pilgrimage.[1] More recently, in an article on death in *The Westminster Dictionary of Christian Theology*, Paul Badham matter-of-factly asserted that "neither the mediaeval emphasis on fear of death nor the confident hopes of the early Christians are much in evidence today." He continues in this article to point out that "though few churchmen explicitly repudiate belief in a future life, the virtual absence of references to it in modern hymns, prayers, and popular apologetic indicates how little part it plays in the contemporary Christian consciousness."[2]

St. George's Churchyard—Then and Now

The force with which the hope of heaven was traditionally stated by the church (even in relatively recent history) came home to me one morning when I was touring Old Dorchester, the remains of a colonial city near my home. My family and I were walking along with an assorted crowd of Brownies, Cub Scouts, visitors from out of state, and at least one public school teacher—a typical group of Americans. We were listening to the lecture of a young historian employed by the parks department.

As we walked among the antique remains of Old Dorchester, the historian "re-created" the town in our imaginations, taking us out onto the parade grounds and marketplace, where colonial militia met and drilled, and the merchants, buyers and craftsmen mingled. The church at the center of town is now nothing more than a brick tower, forty feet high, in the midst of some woods—the ruins appearing much as they did when they were depicted on the cover of an 1875 issue of *Harpers*. We followed the historian down the grassy nave of the church, out into the churchyard, through the arched door still framed by the ancient brick tower. Outside we paused in a circle around a flat tombstone marking the grave of James Postell. The marble stone bore scars on its rounded edges, testimony of the time British soldiers used it as a chopping block while garrisoned there.

The historian pulled a bit of paper out of his pocket. "Imagine," he said, "that we were there when James Postell was buried. As they lowered him into the ground, these are the words we would have heard from the 1768 *Book of Common Prayer*." In grave tones, and with expansive gestures of mock seriousness, he began: "Man that is born of a woman, hath but a short time to live." The young man adjusted his wire-rimmed glasses, cleared his throat and went on: "In the midst of life we are in death: of whom may we seek for succor, but of Thee, O Lord, who for our sins are justly displeased?" Waving a hand out to the crowd and holding up the bit of paper in the other, he went on—thunder in his voice now: "Thou knowest, Lord, the secrets of our hearts; shut not thy merciful ears to our prayers; but spare us . . . suffer us not at our last hour for any pains of death to fall from thee."

And then he winked.

Why did he wink? It was because he knew very well that he shared a secret with us—all of us, whether from Ohio or the Carolinas, or Timbuktu. James Postell—may he rest in peace—would never in this world understand, but we did. The secret that we shared is simply that we no longer take "otherworldly" sentiments seriously. Ideas about the brevity of life, the just judgment of present sinful life, in short, all that devalues this life and prefers the next world, all that fears lest we jeopardize an eternal state in the enjoyment of a temporal existence—all these topics are simply not a part of common polite, serious conversation. We understand the wink and the mock seriousness because we see the world in a quite different light from the contemporaries of James Postell.

However, we also react strongly, and in our world rather negatively, to this quaint reading from an old prayer book, because it was, after all, a very strong statement. We are tempted to class that reading with all antique and outmoded notions of how life is understood. But it is probably *not* the antiquity that we react against. Because it is probably more accurate to say that—out of the whole range of possible attitudes toward death and temporal existence that men and women have ever espoused—*our* attitude is more typical, and it is the strong Christian sentiment of the 1768 *Book of Common Prayer* that is wildly exceptional.

The church had, after all, brought something altogether new into the world with its attitude toward life, death and resurrection. *We* are the ones who have turned back to the older habits—habits of thought as old as humankind. It is these ancient habits of mind and imagination, not really our modernity, that is offended. But the very fact that we almost all agree to be offended—or more often, amused—by these older expressions of faith shows how far we have moved from that view of life even in the church.

Wedded Bliss and the Eternal Hope

Wedding vows illustrate, in another way, how the church has traditionally taken a vitally important human event and rooted it in the transcendent purpose of life. They also provide us, however, with an instructive look at the fact that a secular "sense" of the world is no longer held back at the door of the church. It finds a place in the front pew, if not in the pulpit.

This summer Ben and Cheryl stood before me to take vows of holy matrimony. Much earlier we had talked about the ceremony—the style and arrangements, and the *words*. Ben and Cheryl were convinced that the older ceremonies had much more of a "weighty" and important sound to them.

When we looked at the words of the traditional English-language ceremony from the Episcopal *Book of Common Prayer*, we read:

Dearly beloved: We are gathered together here in the sight of God and in the face of this company [for an event that is not to be taken lightly, but entered into] reverently, discreetly, advisedly, and in the fear of God.

We also looked at an "updated" version. The differences, at first, were subtle and hardly objectionable, except perhaps for the breezier tone:

Dear Friends, we are here assembled in the presence of God to unite A _____ (groom's name) and B _____ (bride's name) in marriage. The Bible teaches that it is to be a permanent relationship of one man and one woman freely and totally committed to each other as companions for life.

That last statement is perhaps not too bad, notwithstanding the fact that monogamy is actually difficult to establish on purely biblical grounds and that "total commitment" may imply a kind of idolatry which the Bible certainly does not teach. Nonetheless, it calls for the exclusive human commitment of the marriage couple and, in that, it is faithful to the intention of the Bible.

What is missing is undoubtedly the spirit of ultimate gravity which surrounds the older version, the feeling that these proceedings are not simply for the moment but are anchored in eternity and that something or someone stands in judgment of every earthly event, and especially on this occasion. The wedding thereby, on the one hand, is lifted up above the common grind, or else, on the other hand, joins the clutter of our everyday existence, with neither much fear nor much joy to distinguish it.

Ben and I liked the sound of this next passage (Cheryl wasn't in on this conversation):

> I require and charge you both, as ye will answer in the dreadful Day of Judgment, when the secrets of all hearts shall be disclosed, that if either of you knows any impediment why ye may not be lawfully joined together, ye do now confess it.

I suppose I have performed a hundred or so weddings in the course of nearly twenty years of ministry; and never once have these words ended the ceremony, even though that is what they clearly threaten. But there is something here very essential to everything that is going on in a wedding: it reminds us all that these words are not just for the moment, but that things spoken now are remembered at the Judgment Seat of God—that human life and human decisions loom greater than we ever thought. The fleeting moment is deceptive; these events are anchored in eternity.

Now, turning to our modern version, we read the parallel:

> Marriage is a companionship which involves mutual commitment and responsibility. You will share alike in the responsibilities and the

joys of life. When companions share a sorrow the sorrow is halved, and when they share a joy the joy is doubled.

The difference between these two statements is the difference between Mt. Sinai and Madison Avenue, or the difference between the "Ancient of Days" and "Days of Our Lives." One speaks of immense ancient columns and steeples, and the other of numerous diplomas hung on the wall behind a psychiatrist's couch.

Another more recent version runs as follows:

I require and charge you both, as you hope for joy and peace in the marriage state. . . .

The words, notice well, *as you hope for joy and peace in the marriage state*, are a precise substitute in this ceremony for the words *as ye will answer in the dreadful Day of Judgment*. This parallel is extremely interesting. We would have to see almost immediately that whoever wrote this paraphrase found it either more tasteful or more convincing to refer to rewards in terms of this life and specifically excised the reference to final judgment.[3]

Along with the focus upon happiness and fulfillment in this life, we find another important comparison. Looking at the requirements of the old vows, we find that they are simple, few and well defined:

Wilt thou have this woman to be thy wedded wife, to live together after God's ordinance, in the holy estate of matrimony?

Turning to the requirements of the newer soul-care version, in contrast, we find them not only difficult to precisely define, but probably utterly impossible to keep:

Will you commit yourself to her happiness and self-fulfillment as a person, and to her usefulness in God's kingdom?

These last words help us to discover the real paradox of our situation. The more intently we focus on our present life (denying, by implication, the transcendent view of life) the more we set ourselves increasingly impossible tasks. A couple can, after all, live together if they have to— and the more they feel they have to, the more likely they will. But to commit oneself to the happiness and self-fulfillment of another (for all its this-worldly sound) is probably to set oneself a godlike agenda for life. One can be faithful to a spouse in terms of sexual fidelity—millions of people have, in spite of the fact that many have failed to be. One can stand by a spouse in illness, poverty, disappointment, grief—millions do it, many of them with admirable courage. And even with the high rate of divorce there are still many more who stay married "till death us do part." All of these promises are well within the range of human possibility.

But when husbands and wives set for themselves the goal of making each other happy—or when one demands of the other that he or she be made happy by this marriage—then disappointment, resentment, frustration, and anger are almost inevitable. It follows that if one is not happy, he or she might well suspect that something is wrong with the marriage. After all, when marriage vows are stripped of their connection with an "eternal destiny" that has become difficult for modern sentiment to embrace, then it becomes a *quid pro quo* contract—a vow given now in view of the happiness promised in the course of time. Marriage is therefore no longer a promise, the issue of which is really decided in eternity. Instead, it is instituted for the purpose of making us happy, loved, fulfilled and significant human beings in this present life.

Heaven and the Modern Church

If the church has weakened and diluted its transcendent vision, as these examples indicate, then what we are seeing here is more than a doctrinal miscalculation or a temporary neglect of a subject that now needs to be addressed. Instead, it is a failure that points toward an essential resistance in the church to that which is at the very heart of its message.

In two fundamental teachings of Christianity we are able to see why the message is called gospel—or good news. And in each case we can see that where the church holds strongly to these teachings, there is also a rise in the general longing and affection for heaven. On other occasions, where heaven is resisted, we should not be surprised that these doctrines as well are met with bewilderment or outright opposition, and a preference for interpreting life from a nontranscendent point of view.

One has to do with the idea of creation, and it is the conviction that creation is a gift, a very good gift from a loving God. The other has to do with the idea of reconciliation: specifically, that the way to salvation is by grace, that it also is a gift from God. Let me briefly explore the connections of these two important ideas with the doctrine of heaven.

1. *Creation is a good gift.*

In much of pagan mythology creation is something wrested out of a primal chaos. The resulting order was sometimes good and sometimes tainted with a curse, the curse being experienced in the various problems attendant to living in the world. For instance, in early Greek cosmogonic myth (myth about creation) sexuality is seen as a curse: it is a mythic explanation of the problems arising because there are two different sexes in humanity. Zeus blighted human beings by dividing them in two—thus weakening their threat to the gods. In other words, the evil that occurs in the world is "in the system." Moral evil is added on to the evil of creation, and is in part explained by creation.

In the biblical story of creation, God created all things *good* (Gen 1:4, 10, 12, 18, 21, 25, 31). Evil is not explained by creation itself, but by the misuse and disorder of creation in the fall of Adam and Eve. Therefore, everything that has come from God is very good, just as God himself is good and has every good intention toward his creation. The Fall never entirely destroys that good; for it is clear that life still centers in that which is given by God. And all that is simply given by God is altogether good.

Now this brings us to the dualism of biblical cosmology. Almost any time the Bible depicts creation, it refers to it as "the heavens and the earth" or "heaven and earth." In part this refers to the natural appearance of the heavens (or the sun, moon and stars—all that is above us) and the earth (all that is below us). But, as Karl Barth pointed out, the habitual dualism of the biblical expression of creation is not without meaning beyond its literal and direct one.

"Earth" is that part of creation that is within our power and under human dominion. "Heaven" is that part of creation in which God himself exercises dominion, and which we do not know intimately until we are at last fully reconciled to God. Therefore, heaven is that part of creation which we can only receive as opposed to that which we control, employ, manipulate and exploit. It is the realm of grace, for it comes entirely as God's gift and represents the fullness of all gifts. Among other things heaven represents an aspect of reality that we can only know and respond to in terms of adoration; we can in no sense possess it. Therefore our response to things of this earth is properly thanksgiving, and our response to the matters of heaven, praise.

This dualism of heaven and earth tells us two important things about the way we relate to creation. The first is that human action is a response to creation, and it does not constitute reality. (We cannot really "become as gods.") We might imagine that the whole earth responds to our wills, but in saner hours we know that is not the case.

Even if we affect a small part of the earth, our actions are fraught with all kinds of ambiguity. Our intentional efforts to do a good thing, for instance, always invite the possibility of unintended evil. We work hard to enrich human life and, destroying the environment, threaten the possibility of life itself. We give to the poor and undermine their self-reliance. We make a better product and destroy our neighbors' livelihood. We are everywhere faced with the sobering realization that we cannot create the world, or even re-create it; we can only respond to that which God has given.

Biblical cosmology relates that fact to us on a cosmic scale. If even the visible creation stands always somewhat aloof from our exertions to make it bend to our wills, then how much more does that part of creation which lies beyond our senses. Creation includes that which responds to the will of God alone. And that is called heaven.

Furthermore, the second important insight that comes from this realization of heaven is that the world does not find its purpose in itself. Jürgen Moltmann used the term "eccentric"—the reality of heaven means that the world does not center in itself, it centers in God. It is eccentric because it centers outside of itself. Thus the reality of the earth is found in its relationship to that which is outside of itself. This insight applies to more than cosmology. It applies to everything: all things find their reality in God—not because they are illusory, but because they are created in relationship. In God "we live and move and have our being" (Acts 17:28). Reality is relationship. John said it this way: "God is love" (1 Jn 4:8).

2. *Salvation comes by grace.*

Now we can see that a world closed in upon itself, dependent on nothing outside itself—in short, a nontranscendent world—must understand existence altogether differently from a world believing strongly in a transcendent order. For a world that is open to the mystery of heaven is, first of all, a world that believes in the possibility of grace. It is true that the confidence of a nontranscendent world comes from its self-reliance, but so does its despair.

Curiously, a world that believes it is always subject to the mystery of heaven has less to say about self-reliance but shows decidedly more confidence. It is a world predisposed to expect help.

Children instinctively expect grace; so children's stories often center on the gift that makes the ugly duckling a swan, the unwanted stepdaughter a princess, the department-store Santa turn out to be real. Near disasters turn inside out and prove the triumph of good over evil. J. R. R. Tolkein called that fictional device "eucatastrophe"—a good catastrophe.

When my daughter was three and a half years old, she had become a fan of Judy Garland's classic film *The Wizard of Oz*. During that same year, an elderly neighbor, whose fond attention and lively wit had endeared him to my children, became ill and, after a few weeks, died. It was a time for questions about the catastrophes of life, and she began asking about death.

"How do people get to heaven after they die?" Emily asked one morning over breakfast.

"I don't really know *how*," I confessed, and then stumbled through some lame explanation that God knows the answer, even if we don't and that we should be satisfied with that. She was not satisfied, I could tell.

Suddenly, her pensive mood changed. "Maybe it's like when Dorothy was going back to Kansas," she said brightly.

"How's that?" I asked.

"Don't you remember? She just clicked her heels together and said, 'There's no place like home. There's no place like home.' " Grace in a child's story and grace in the real-life triumph over disaster—each calls forth the same sentiment, that life is overshadowed by a benevolent mystery.

As adults grow in their strength over the world, they lose that sense of grace that is so keenly felt by children. Children at first earn nothing and are given everything. Gradually they learn that their environment must be mastered, that elements of life must be earned; at some point it will be called "making a living." It's important for them to learn that lesson, for that is being "responsible." It is a *response* to the gift of life.

But at the same time it is natural that they should eventually lose sight of how much they are dependent on what is simply given—what they can in no sense earn. They focus on "making a living" and forget that the object of making a living is life and that life is never earned; it is only given.

Jesus said, "Unless you change and become like little children, you will never enter the kingdom of heaven." The meaning of these words become clear when we see that our immediate (childlike) perception of life as grace is, at every turn, submerged by our growing power over the world. As children we receive the world; as adults our focus narrows to that which we have constructed by our own effort. The huge gift is forgotten, while our minuscule response becomes a source of obsession, pride, anxiety, envy, guilt and fear.

All this tells us is that our experience of the world moves us toward one or the other of opposing attitudes. Either life is a gift, or it is a product of my will. The more we move toward that latter expression of life, the more the absolute necessity of grace eludes us. The world shrinks and becomes only a complex of responses to ourselves. We necessarily live between these polar attitudes, with always the distinct danger that we will lose sight of the former in pursuit of the latter.

The Earth's "Darkling Plain" and the Eclipse of Heaven

Here we can begin to see why the loss of a sense of heaven "over us" is more than a shift in cosmological theory, or in the way we picture the world in our minds.[4] Instead it has to do with the way we live in the light of heaven. During a solar eclipse, which I have witnessed twice, the earliest noticeable effect (long before total eclipse) is that the whole atmosphere is shrouded in an eerily dimming light. I think we witness a similar effect in the loss of a sense of transcendence, though our souls (like our eyes) accommodate the darkness at first too easily.

Long before the present stage of eclipse, the nineteenth-century poet Matthew Arnold thought of the retreating realm of faith as he listened to the ebb and flow of waves upon Dover Beach. There was a time, his verse suggests, when the "Sea of Faith" was at high tide casting a bright shadow over all existence; but now one only hears "its melancholy, long withdrawing roar" and the shores of the earth are left "naked shingles." The result is loss of moral certainty or confidence in a world ruled by ultimate good and illuminated by grace:

> And we are here as on a darkling plain
> Swept with confused alarms of struggle and flight,
> Where ignorant armies clash by night.[5]

Arnold intuitively caught the essence of a world left without a vision of the transcendent: a world of struggles without victory and of sacrifice without purpose.

These matters are not fully appreciated, however, unless we attempt to recall how the church—and indeed the world—once experienced the bright, overshadowing reality of heaven.

CHAPTER 3

THE BRIGHT SHADOW
OF HEAVEN

Two loves therefore have given original to
these two cities—self-love in contempt of
God unto the earthly; love of God in
contempt of one's self to the heavenly.

Augustine of Hippo

• • •

WE HAVE SEEN THAT MODERN LIFE IS MARKED BY A LOSS OF A SENSE OF TRAN-
scendence. The examples I used could be multiplied a thousand times,
because the fading light of heaven is an experience that pervades everything, all our institutions, our manners and our philosophies. We cannot
fully appreciate what difference this makes, however, without thinking
seriously about the meaning and implications of a vigorous sense of the
transcendent.

Let's imagine a time such as that—one that contrasts with our loss
of transcendence in modern Western life. What would it be like? How
would people so affected think and feel? What difference, if any, would
it make in the way they live?

One November afternoon a few years ago I stood before a series of
maps mounted on an ancient wall near the center of Rome. The maps

depicted the advancing frontier of the Roman Empire from its beginnings in central Italy down to the time it spanned the known world. I tried to think what it must have been like there, in that very place, within sight of the Roman Forum, only a stone's throw from the Colosseum, and within a brief walk of the Palatine, where Caesars built their palatial houses. Roman power, Roman law, tying together the far-flung provinces of an empire, centered upon what was, even at that time, called the "Eternal City." In that place one could sense the awe with which pilgrims from the outlying provinces glimpsed the huge buildings, the architectural symbols of imperial might. Even late in the empire, the saying was repeated:

As long as the Coliseum stands
Rome shall stand
When the Coliseum falls,
Rome will fall,
When Rome falls,
The world will fall.[1]

The Romans of that time would not have seen what I saw—ruins on every side. The ancient Forum had long since been gutted of most of its marble. The Coliseum was vacant, partially collapsed for centuries now—a fabulous ruin, but a ruin nevertheless. The Circus Maximus, where Roman society gathered for some of its most splendid occasions, was a bare contoured field, almost in the shadow of the Palatine where the homes of the greatest Romans have now vanished like early morning mist on the hills of central Italy.

No one saw this at the time, I say. No one, that is, except the Christians.

They had seen that there is something eternal, something greater than life on earth, but it was not Rome. They had it engrafted into their hearts and minds that all earthly things must finally crumble and fall. What comes from nothing, returns to nothing. This perspective, though held only by a minority of the people in the Roman world, began a revolution in perspective toward time, life, death and eternity. The intensity and character of their conviction—very different as we will see from the simple pagan hope for life after death—left an indelible impression upon society for centuries to come.

In choosing to use this time as a sort of comparison to the epoch we now experience, I am not encouraging a cult of "pristine Christianity." We should have no illusions, in the first place, that human problems then, even in the life of the church, were not as serious as ours. On the contrary, I am convinced that where those ancient people were wrong, they were quite as wrong as we are. I could not forget, for instance, Tertullian's gleeful vision, in one sermon, of pagans burning in hell while Christians watched with smug satisfaction. Such excesses seem less than Christian, I think, because there is none of the spirit of Christ in it. That is not to say that Tertullian was not a brilliant, gifted, and very great Christian, but only that he suffered from cultural blindness just as we do. Nevertheless, I think we will not go wrong in looking at these first centuries in the Christian experience for four reasons. (1) It incorporates the time in which the New Testament was produced. And that little bundle of documents is the most important measure of Christian thought and life in every age. It is the base from which everything has been measured, so we are hardly arbitrary in comparing our time to the time these writings were produced. (2) It is obviously a time in which a concept of the world changed dramatically, and in that regard is like our own time. (3) Its emerging emphasis upon the transcendent (even to the point of courting martyrdom) is quite as striking as our nontranscendent world view. Finally, (4) it was obviously a time that powerfully affected culture and society, especially in the West, but ultimately throughout the world: we still feel the winds that began to blow out of Asia in that era.

The Taste for Eternity

Our own cultural bias probably causes us to miss what was remarkable about those early days of Christian expansion. We would be tempted to see the whole enterprise as "successful," noticing how rapidly the movement spread. But that criterion would probably not occur to them, or at least would seem to be a peculiarly one-dimensional way of describing what was happening. They undoubtedly thought at times that the persecution of the church was taking more Christians out of the world than they were taking into the church. But this fact made no material difference, because their confidence was based upon a hope of reality that transcended anything that might happen in history.

Of all the New Testament writers, only Luke seems to have taken any note of the growing numbers of Christians. And, even at that, his interest is obviously not in Christianity's appeal to the masses, but in its power to overcome all obstacles—something which is only illustrated in the growing numbers of new believers. For Luke, like all the other writers of New Testament Scripture, felt that the issues of life are not really settled here but in eternity. The book of Acts, therefore, ends not with optimistic forecasts, but with unbelieving disputants being judged by the words of Isaiah.

The words of John's Epistle were the very essence of this Christian view of life: "Do not love the world or anything in the world. . . . For everything in the world—the cravings of sinful man, the lust of his eyes and the boasting of what he has and does—comes not from the Father but from the world. The world and its desires pass away, but the man who does the will of God lives forever" (1 Jn 2:15-17). However Christians might have differed on a number of topics, their attitude toward the world, its impermanence, and the altogether greater importance of eternity was the very fulcrum from which they succeeded in moving the world.

The teachings of Jesus that come through to us in the Gospels reflect this same warning against impermanence. Beware of laying up your treasures on earth, where thieves, moth, and rust take them away. Remember the man who filled his barn with provisions, and thought he had done all—just before he died. Remember the one who built his house upon the sand.

The Gospels are also permeated with sayings such as "Do not set your heart on what you will eat or drink; do not worry about it. . . . But seek [God's] kingdom" (Lk 12:29, 31); "Do not be afraid of those who kill the body but cannot kill the soul. Rather, be afraid of the One who can destroy both soul and body in hell" (Mt 10:28); "Sell your possessions and give to the poor. Provide purses for yourselves that will not wear out, a treasure in heaven that will not be exhausted. . . . For where your treasure is, there your heart will be also" (Lk 12:33-34). To recite a great list of these sayings would be tedious and unnecessary; it is obvious that to take these references to the transcendent aim of life out of the gospel would be to render the life and teachings of Jesus unrecognizable.

In the face of Corinth teachers' saying "there is no resurrection of the dead," the apostle Paul made the point explicit. The gospel is founded upon the reality of Christ's resurrection, and his resurrection means our resurrection. Without this we have no hope and, furthermore, he said to the Corinthian Christians, "you are still in your sins" (1 Cor 15:17). Without this resurrection, there is no gospel. It is not what happens in this life alone that justifies the gospel, but that which remains utterly outside this life.

Extending their focus upon eternity into the next two generations, we see that these words and many others like them made the greatest impression imaginable upon the developing church, capturing the imagination of the world around. Though the historian Gibbon tended to state the matter in terms of its effect in dissolving classical culture, he saw clearly the character and importance of this kind of teaching to the early church. Something new appeared with the Christians, Gibbon said, and it was a confident, all-absorbing belief that the fortunes of this world count for nothing at all next to the reality of the coming judgment of all peoples.

Athanasius, perhaps the best spokesman of his age on the spirit of the Christian movement, sees victory over death as the center of Christian confidence. Death no longer terrifies those in the church, he says, but is put in its place. The proof of this is that death is now "despised by all Christ's disciples, and that they all take the aggressive against it and no longer fear it; but by the sign of the cross and by faith in Christ tread it down as dead."[2] The resurrection of Christ had destroyed what was formerly an insurmountable barrier—an absolute limit. Now Christians overwhelm every barrier: not fearing death, they fear nothing at all. The filling ranks of martyrs are more than ample evidence, claimed Athanasius, of the boldness and strength of the church. "For while in tender years they made haste to die, and not men only, but women also." Death has been conquered, bound hand and foot at the cross. Now "all they who are in Christ, as they pass by, trample on him and, witnessing to Christ, scoff at death, jesting at him and saying what has been written against him of old: 'O death, where is thy victory? O grave, where is thy sting?' "[3]

It is important that in Athanasius' writings, as in most of the church fathers, the emphasis is not on speculation concerning life after death but on the amazing transformation of attitudes toward death. At one time the world cringed in terror before death, engaging in timid dreams of continued life, of wisps and shades of remaining vitality. But the coming of Christ was like the sun rising over the dark horizon: the shadows of fear, dread and terror fled at the blazing brilliance of the One who triumphed over death.

Athanasius writes in the midst of a world where the vitality of this new attitude was still clearly felt. There was no genuine attraction in the pagan dreams of holding onto life: but this was something quite different. It was the willingness to give up life, to literally defy death. It was not the dream of preserving some semblance of existence, but of suddenly being energized by the prospect of giving oneself unreservedly to God who is stronger than death. It was not a holding on with fear to life but a letting go in defiance of death. It was a passion for life, because the fear of death had been overcome. "For when one sees men, weak by nature," Athanasius said, "leaping forward to death, and not fearing its corruption nor frightened of the descent to Hades, but with eager soul challenging it, and not flinching from torture, but on the contrary, for Christ's sake electing to rush upon death in preference to life upon earth," then any person can see that it is Christ himself who "gives to each the victory over death."[4]

New Life and the Death of Death

For reasons that will become apparent I want to underscore what was different in this Christian hope of eternal life from the ordinary pagan dream of immortality. It is a distinction that has become blurred, I think, in our own time, but that was evidently important to early Christians. Tatian, though finally declared a heretic, speaks well enough for orthodox thought on this point. He insisted that Christianity was not simply a repetition of pagan wishes for personal survival. He often became so intent upon refuting the typical Greek idea of immortality that he even argued that Christians have no hope of personal survival, only the hope of being taken up into the life of God.

He put the case perhaps more strongly than others, but he found himself having to refute the habitual notion that eternal life means the natural immortality of the soul. Essentially, he saw this continued existence as only a prolonging of the self-centered life, an immortality that ignores our absolute dependence upon God. The Christian view toward death was, after all, both positive and negative. Death was to be desired in the first place, in that it frees us from sin. That is why the cross stands at the center of the Christian life. It is why Jesus said, "Whoever wants to save his life will lose it, but whoever loses his life for me will find it" (Mt 16:25).

The contrast, as Tatian saw it, consisted in the Christian willingness to face death. His Greek-thinking contemporaries, Tatian knew, were tempted to take up one of two attitudes toward death: they either feared death or denied it. The Christian, on the other hand, both affirmed its reality and believed that God had conquered death. "After losing immortality," Tatian said, "men have conquered death by submitting to death in faith."[5] The pagan hopes for a continuation of the same life; the Christian's hope arises from the possibility of a new life within a new relationship to God. The pagan wish might be represented as a grasping

after more life, whereas Christianity is a letting go of life for the sake
of receiving that new gift from God. "Why is it your fate," he said to
the philosophers of his age, "to go on grasping for things and to go on
dying over and over again? Die to the world, and repudiate its madness.
Live to God, take hold of Him, and lay aside your old nature."[6] It fell
to Tatian and to his teacher, Justin Martyr, perhaps more than other
Christian writers of that time, to stress the difference between Christian and Greek ideas of immortality. As Jaroslav Pelikan in his fine little
book *The Shape of Death* pointed out, there were other Christians, such
as Clement of Alexandria, who stressed the similarities of Christian
hope and the general idea of immortality. Nevertheless, Christians
found that ultimately the gospel itself demanded that the cross (and the
reality and seriousness of death) be the prior condition to resurrection.
No cross, no crown. Thus the hope for immortality could never become
an escape from death, based upon some natural possibilities within life,
but must always be a hope that rested only upon God.

Theologians have struggled with the distinction between immortality
and the Christian hope of resurrection. Generally the difference can be
stated this way: In the pagan idea of immortality, life is possessed of the
quality or power to continue even beyond death. The Christian hope,
however, always centered upon God. Thus, to say we believe in immortality is not incorrect as long as we understand it as a gift, a condition
made possible by God's raising us to new life.

Therefore, the central and abiding distinction in Christianity is not
merely a hope of immortality—only one more variety of the same kind
of wish. What we have here, clearly, is the birth of a *new center of gravity*.
Before that the balance had existed within the world; now it was utterly
outside. For it is God who raises us from the dead, just as it is God who
gives us each new moment of life.

Now we can begin to understand the rush of vitality that suddenly
overwhelmed the Mediterranean world. The dynamic was not born, and
could never have been born, of the satisfaction of that ancient wish for
immortality. That desire has some relationship, I would think, to what

took place. But by comparison to the energy and the new life that pulsed throughout the Christian movement, that old sentiment was only an impoverished shadow. It was perhaps only a vacuum that this Christian hope of resurrection had filled up. Paul compared them as shadow and substance when he said to the Corinthians that the Christian life amounts to this:

> Meanwhile we groan, longing to be clothed with our heavenly dwelling, because when we are clothed, we will not be found naked. For while we are in this tent, we groan and are burdened, because we do not wish to be unclothed but to be clothed with our heavenly dwelling, so that what is mortal may be swallowed up by life. (2 Cor 5:2-4)

The Practical Evidence of Eternity

Thus it is not enough to say that Christians of the New Testament era, and of the succeeding generations, believed in the resurrection of the dead, or in heaven. That would have been insignificant without the fact that their belief was demonstrated in life. The evidence of this new orientation toward life and death was, according to account after account, a change in the very manner of life—a new strength to live in a way that countered the very current of the ancient civilizations, to live in modesty, industry, charity and purity in a world obsessed by pride, consumption, envy, gluttony and sexual license.

Athanasius' most important proof of the resurrection of Christ from the dead was this: look how *these* people live in *this* world. Here is the work of a living Savior, he says: "drawing men to religion, persuading to virtue . . . leading on to a desire for heavenly things . . . imparting strength to meet death." The power of virtue is linked to a new orientation, a sense of the transcendent in the midst of life: "every unruly pleasure is checked, and everyone is looking up from earth to heaven."[7]

The great fourth-century Bishop of Alexandria was not the only one to link these two remarkable features of the Christian movement. The reports from contemporary sources were so consistent in this regard that the historian Gibbon, in the famous fifteenth and sixteenth chapters of his _Decline and Fall of the Roman Empire,_ saw these qualities as the powerful solvent that he thought eventually brought the collapse of classical culture. Though he is primarily drawn to the excesses of Christian apocalyptic expectations, he rightly detects the importance of this teaching in the early church and the dramatic impact early Christians had upon the pagan culture. The pagan intimations of immortality were vague and weak, more speculation than conviction. By contrast, the "error," as Gibbon termed it, of the Christians "was productive of the most salutary effects on the faith and practice of Christians, who lived in the awful expectation of that moment when the globe itself, and all the various race of mankind, should tremble at the appearance of their divine judge."[8]

Contemporary Christian writings bear out Gibbon's estimate. Midway in the second century, Justin Martyr confidently appeals to the emperor Pius in the following terms:

Before we became Christians, we took pleasure in debauchery, now we rejoice in purity of life; we used to practice magic and sorcery, now we are dedicated to the good, unbegotten God; we used to value above all else money and possessions, now we bring together all that we have and share it with those who are in need. Formerly, we hated and killed one another and, because of a difference in nationality or custom, we refused to admit strangers within our gates. Now since the coming of Christ we all live in peace. We pray for our enemies and seek to win over those who hate us unjustly in order that . . . they may partake with us in the same joyful hope.[9]

The psychology of this new attitude toward life and death we can now begin to understand. For, essentially, Christians have found something to die _for;_ therefore, they had also found something to live for. Life was no longer a possession one longed to preserve, but it was what one desired to devote to God. Life could not be captured. It could only be experienced truly in relationship—that is, in love. A paradox stands at the center of life: only when we give it away, do we really have it. That was the secret that was hidden in the life, death and resurrection of

Christ. There is, therefore, no longer any threat from death; it cannot take from a person what he has already willingly given up. And since he has given it up to God, he has expended life in pursuit of its truest and highest aims.

In a book about her near-fatal illness, Marsha Spradlin concluded that what she experienced as the fear of dying "was not the fear of dying at all, but the sorrow of never having lived with a purpose."[10] An honest appraisal of this, in ourselves, will almost always bring us to the same conclusion. It is not simply the length of life, but the "why" of life that begs for an answer. And it is not a question that easily yields to a promise of more-of-the-same.

Of course, the reason Christians believed in the resurrection of the dead was that Jesus Christ was raised, historically and bodily, from the dead. It is upon that concrete event that their confidence was built. But the *meaning* of the resurrection is more than assurance of personal survival; it means that the life given to God can, in no sense, be lost.

The Christian Meaning of Transcendence

What I am now about to say, I think, is already suggested by this marked distinction in the Christian view of eternal life that we have just discerned. The pagan desire for immortality could not be expected to change human behavior, but the Christian hope did. To desire more of what you already have is one thing; but to stand ready to expend life, to throw it overboard for the sake of something greater than you now have, is quite a different matter. The one is centered in self; the other is centered in God.

I have mentioned a recent essay in *Time* that cited statistics showing that most Americans still believe in heaven—and by a healthy majority. A similar poll in Europe revealed basically the same tendency there.[11] However, as Helen Oppenheimer pointed out, "People who simply want to rebuild the agreeable life they know in heaven are, precisely, worldly."[12] Thus, the mere belief that we will survive death—which amounts to the denial of death—does not mean that we adhere to the strong

Christian sense of transcendence.

Unlike the common pagan wish for life beyond death, the Christian hope for heaven answers not so much to our desire to *have life without limit* as it does our deeply felt need to *give life without restraint.* This sense of transcendence, which underlay so much of the moral and creative energy of our civilization for centuries, and which even now must be present in authentic Christianity, is marked by two qualities.

The first is that it imparts the courage to live. This is why Paul refers to the presence of the Holy Spirit as the "earnest" of the Spirit: here was a living, God-given assurance in this life of that which is the end and goal of life. The presence of the Spirit means that one has already entered into life and that death is no longer *only* a future issue to be faced with trepidation and fear. The issue of death has already been settled. "In Christ's death," Augustine said, "death died . . . the fullness of life swallowed up death; death was absorbed in the body of Christ."[13] The Christian, without denying death, recognizes something greater than death. Therefore, he is not afraid to live.

Release from the Prison of Self
The second quality marking a Christian sense of transcendence is love.

To the extent Christian teachings ever appealed to a sense of transcendence, it was a thoroughgoing transcendence. It was not simply about a life beyond this life or even a world beyond this world. But it was a Thou beyond this I, one that is only realized when we get outside ourselves and see the other. That is why the whole matter centered on love: because love is grounded in, and as a matter of fact only speaks of, relationship. And relationship involves an I and a Thou. Nontranscendence truly is when the whole of being threatens to collapse into the "I," and no "Thou" is possible. And transcendence is when the "I" opens out in love toward a true "other"—a "Thou."

I am using Martin Buber's language, of course, when I speak of the I-Thou: that "primary word" as he called it. But as can clearly be seen, this sentiment was firmly embedded in Christianity from the beginning.

Jesus was in one sense, as Albert Schweitzer realized, an apocalyptic teacher. Like more than a few others, in first-century Israel, he was preaching of the end; he was preaching of the kingdom of God. But he also pressed the ethical and theological importance of this "fullness of time" further than anyone ever had. The nature of his ministry, in a few words, consisted in demonstrating that the New Era, the New Kingdom—this messianic expectation—did not only cut into time, dividing one time from another. It penetrated to the heart of every moment one lived. He showed the transcendence at the core of every relationship.

It can be seen in the fact that all of his apocalyptic teachings were ethical teachings—all of them, without exception. They were not speculation about the end, nor visions to fascinate idle curiosity. But they were teachings on faithfulness to the end, steadfastness, courage, service and love: the servant remaining faithful to his absent master, the wisdom of the bridal party, the prudence of the servants who have investments to make, the love of those who meet every day with the ill, the stranger and the imprisoned (see Mt 24—25). Each moment in life confronts us with the end of life.

One day the world itself will be turned inside-out, so that we will know the truth of the world. But in truth, for those who see it, it is happening now. "The kingdom of God is within you" (Lk 17:21). That is why you must take up your cross, losing your life-unto-death for the sake of death-unto-life. Everything is related to that end—on the personal level as well as the cosmic level. Therefore the true story of the judgment is this:

When the Son of man shall appear with all his angels, he will divide the peoples of the earth like dividing sheep from goats. And he will say to those on his right hand, "Come, you who are blessed by my Father; take your inheritance, the kingdom prepared for you since the creation of the world. For I was hungry and you gave me something to eat, I was thirsty and you gave me something to drink. . . . I was in prison and you came to visit me" (Mt 25:31-36).

And there will be our startled reply: "When did we see you in prison?"

We are startled because we do not yet understand about the kingdom. And we do not yet understand that if heaven can be found anywhere, it can be found even in prison.

*　　*　　*

Let me state the issue this way: *To discover heaven, we must answer the invitation to step outside of ourselves. Another human being is that invitation.*

Teaching a course on Plato at a state prison, I had an unexpected meeting of minds with one of the inmates. Normally I was there for a couple of hours, once a week, in the evening. Anxious to get home from a long day, this being the last of several events, I would hurriedly pull together my notes, pack my books, walk briefly to the main gate and check myself through the three guard points, then head for home.

Something had been happening to one of the students, a man in his late twenties whom we will call Steve, while reading Plato. I cannot tell why I know, but in the course of *The Republic*, something new began to take place, a new intensity in Steve's reading and conversation. One evening while discussing how Plato connected the ideas of the just city and the well-ordered soul, I could see him sitting bolt upright. He was devouring the subject now—it was as if he remembered or recognized something. Maybe I noticed because I recall the time when I saw the same kind of thing myself. From that day on, Steve's reading took fire. He came to class prepared—more than prepared, doubly and triply prepared.

What desperate crime Steve had committed to be imprisoned I don't know. I didn't ask. And he didn't talk about it. But whatever it was, I had the impression that he suddenly became aware of his own true guilt, not just his legal guilt—but his moral responsibility and therefore, also, his own "original goodness," as Kant would have called it.

Several times he came forward to talk further after class. As I've said, I was usually thinking about going home, putting up my notes, checking through the gates, where guards seemed in no great hurry to deliver me to the outside.

In my concern for the next thing I did not attend to the "first things," nor did I fully recognize that here—once again—was an invitation, a glimpse of that world outside of myself. And this is the very essence of that sense of transcendence. Occasionally it would occur to me that he was a student (not the typical college student, but not as far from one as you might guess) who was genuinely interested in learning—not the most common thing for the 1980s. I would stop for a moment, and we would talk, sometimes carrying on the conversation out into the brightly lit courtyard, where you could just dimly see the stars. He had a family—much like mine, as a matter of fact, with children about the same ages. He told me of their visit at Thanksgiving. His son did well in school; he made the principal's list as I recall, every term. Nothing would, or should, have moved me to sympathy more than his talks about his family. We would talk often until a guard walked up to tell us the courtyard was closed. The interruption was not entirely unwelcome: as I said, I was also anxious to be on my way.

Who was this young man? Often I thought of the youthful wayward-ness of great saints who had suddenly been turned by a provident en-counter with the truth. Steve left Plato to read St. Augustine. Of course, St. Augustine was no criminal, except in his own eyes. But the kind of conversion that the Bishop of Hippo describes in *Confessions* may have been similar. He had read Cicero's *Hortensius*, which he later saw as a kind of preparation for the more weighty truth of the gospel.

Now and then it occurs to me who Steve was—in his real, historical, concrete, criminal and saintly existence. He was someone *other* than my-self, who demanded my attention. Out of intensity of interest? Ambi-tion? Curiosity? I don't know. I only know that because of any number of pure, or tangled reasons, he wanted to stop me in my haste and invite me to step outside of myself. Our conversations were engaging, friend-ly, humorous, well versed in Plato and Augustine—and, except for one or two occasions, very brief. To my shame, it occurred to me that if I took him to be someone more important I might have been more accom-modating.

But if I had paid more attention to Matthew 25, I would have known who he was. My own loss of a sense of transcendence had betrayed me.

What is behind this central New Testament idea of meeting Christ in strangers, and prisoners, and the ill? What does it mean?

Eternal Life as Freedom

Let me answer this question by drawing from what we have already observed. That is, does it now become clear that those very features that so energized early Christians, and that drew them to works of compassion and to a disciplined life, are also involved in my relationship to another human being?

For instance, the freedom to live courageously in the face of death is the same kind of liberation that occurs when I am no longer burdened by the necessity of maintaining what I call my own: my time, my possessions, my prestige or my plans. It is the freedom from having to protect and justify my life.

"It is for freedom that Christ has set us free," the apostle Paul said (Gal 5:1), and by that expression he identified a central feature of the Christian experience—being set free from the burden of sin, with its self-centeredness and its demands for self-justification.

Steve gave me an opportunity to free myself of a burden. In this case the burden was my schedule, my time, which was weighing heavily upon me. For a moment, attending to him, enjoying his conversation, I would step outside the world of *my* time, *my* self-imposed demands and enter freely into the world of another human experience. It is only as I enter into the freedom of another life that the exclusive demands of justifying my own life fall away, leaving me free for the experience of life as a pure and simple gift from God. Here is precisely the source of courage against death that Athanasius described so eloquently; to the extent we have already died to the burden of self-will and self-justification, we have become free to live.

Eternal Life as Love

The fear of death—or the fear of giving oneself for the sake of another—conceives of life as a possession. Life must be spared from danger and from competing interests of another human being.

It is a life at war for survival. Fellowship can be based on the maxim "The enemy of my enemy is my friend" or upon the associations of family and tribe that are needed for survival. But essentially life must be protected; therefore it is isolated from relationships with others. Jesus saw this as an illusion of life—death disguising itself as life. Thus he said, "Whoever wants to save his life will lose it" (Mt 16:25).

The gospel, however, is based on a different idea about life. Life is not a possession to be hoarded, but a dynamic openness toward the world and others. It is seeing, hearing, conversing and sharing. It is the giving of oneself openly to another. It is love. Life, understood this way, recognizes that relationship is at the heart of all being. Thus God is seen as Trinity: his unity is not in isolated individuality, but it is a unity of community.[14] The first letter of John declares "God is love"—that is the essential character of God. So those who fail to share life, lose it; in rejecting relationship (out of fear, pride, ambition, greed) they have rejected life, for life *is* relationship.

When we see this, of course, we cannot miss the point that the reality of heaven means even the world itself is not centered in itself. Instead, it centers in its own transcendent goal—it centers in heaven. Therefore, to say that the world has a purpose is to say that its essential meaning is relationship. All things exist for this life in and of the other, for relationship and ultimately for the glory of God.

The biblical description of fallen humanity always involves the loss of relationship. The threat to Cain was that he be hidden from God's presence, estranged from all peoples and exiled from the land. "My punishment," said Cain, "is more than I can bear." God's threat was a mortal threat. For Cain's crime, every form of relationship stood under the curse. And the ultimate expression of losing relationship is death.

The powerful insight that life *is* relationship animates stories such as *Silas Marner*, in which a small girl, Eppie, succeeds in winning the heart of a miser, whose life had been locked tight, protecting his fortune against a threatening world. The Bible recognizes this as *the* issue in life. The whole issue of life and death is bound up in the recognition of an *other*. Jesus therefore taught that "whoever loses his life for me will find it" (Mt 16:25).

Also bound up with this idea is that of loving action toward another person. Out of fear of losing life (or a part of it) we isolate ourselves against others. But Jesus stands at the boundary of our isolated, individual life and calls upon us to discover relationship—that is, to discover life. This is the paradox involved in Bonhoeffer's famous saying "When Christ calls a man, he bids him come and die."

Eternal Life as Worship

Central to the idea of worship is sacrifice. The biblical critique of the sacrificial systems was that they tended to be made into a substitute for the worshipers' real offering of their own lives to God. But what is the meaning of sacrifice except to divest oneself of possession (the possession of one's best lamb in the flock or the possession of a whole day in the week) in favor of relationship? (The sacrifice becomes a gift to God.) The Christian call to life is one of sacrificing all: "If anyone would come after me, he must deny himself and take up his cross and follow me" (Mt 16:24). Thus the true character of an authentic life is one that is altogether given over to God. It is a life, in Paul's language, lived "in Christ."

This language of sacrifice helps us to discover why Jesus emphasized the imprisoned, the poor, the ill and the outsiders, as if these are particular opportunities to come to him. Here, in these cases, the last opportunity to engage in relationship for the sake of self-promotion is stripped away. Otherwise we might fool ourselves into thinking that we love, when in fact we are only cherishing the thought of what others might do for us. Among the poor and the imprisoned, the opportunity for love is unhindered by ambition and greed.

The nontranscendent view of the world is one in which all things, even relationships, are reduced to the pragmatic. They must answer the question, What's in it for me? The secret of those through the ages who have longed for heaven is that in the simplicity of love given to another, they have glimpsed the splendor of a wholly other world. And like John Wesley, their hearts have been strangely warmed.

CHAPTER 4

AT HOME
IN THE WORLD

A lifetime of happiness! No man could bear it.
It would be hell on earth.

Bernard Shaw, *Man and Superman*

•   •   •

"OTHER WORLD! THERE IS NO OTHER WORLD! HERE OR NOWHERE IS THE WHOLE fact." Ralph Waldo Emerson's words, with their no-nonsense ring and appeal to the spirit of common sense, have not lacked for sympathetic minds at any time since they were written. Why, then, has the church so often, and for so long, resisted this sensible accommodation to the only world we really know? What could possibly be wrong with saying "This world is my home"?

The Domestication of the World
In decided contrast to Emerson, St. John of the Cross said, "God is at home, we are in the far country." That is a statement altogether faithful to the Christian tradition, but it is also an idea that shocks. Such sentiments always have. The difference today is that the idea itself sounds more and more foreign. We are not in the far country, we tell ourselves.

Life—by which we mean this earthly existence—is meant to be satisfying. We hunger for something, and it is here that we should find it, or not at all. Yet when we hunger for career success, large houses, dream vacations, the recognition of our peers, satisfaction is as elusive as ever.

As long as people were taught the idea, as St. John expressed it, that our true home is elsewhere, there was a certain satisfaction in the answer itself. For centuries, the idea that this world is not, by itself, our home—emotionally, spiritually, or even socially—was a compelling idea because it was enormously convincing. It unlocked a secret about human existence that seemed to fit what everyone already sensed about human suffering, human aspirations, and the desire to express life in self-giving love. Neither the flame of persecution nor the ever-present danger of disease or war could extinguish this new lease on life. Nor could the tedium of pots and pans, or the drudgery of daily labor.

Poverty was still painful but not hopeless. Illness might end in death, but death was not the absolute end. Life took on a creative and vibrant energy because it was harnessed to an overall purpose. Never mind the philosophical arguments for life after death; and never mind the speculations concerning heaven, hell, and the last state of the world—this transcendent goal of life opened up new possibilities for *this* world. It was as if a great window were opened and a breeze from that other world stirred through a world that, in antiquity, had turned more and more in upon itself. Its preoccupation with sensuality, power, ambition and death is evident in the first-century Stoic and Epicurean philosophers and in the steady decline of private morals and public order. It was precisely when classical culture seemed to have run out of its earlier cultural vitality that the Christian gospel began to stir new embers; this new breeze blew them to a white heat, until centuries later, they burst into a flame that we now call Western civilization.

What I wish to point out is that the conviction about heaven as our true home, and not earth, answered questions that—in one form or another—will always be there. And when we propose to replace the classic Christian answer, then we must note, first of all, the sort of problems we are tackling. The answers provided by the biblical promise of heaven are given in three principal ways. First, heaven provides adequate room for human hope. Second, it answers the question of suffering. And third, it appeals to our desire for self-transcendence.

Let's look at each of these and see what problems arise when we propose to make this world—and not heaven—our home.

The Transcendence of Hope

Once Jürgen Moltmann, the noted German theologian, showed me a Bible that belonged to him. It wasn't just any Bible. It was a little New Testament, with the Psalms, that was given to him by an American chaplain when he was a prisoner of war in 1945. All around him, among the other prisoners, he found hopelessness and despair. They were aware that many German cities had been reduced to rubble. The economy was in a shambles. Worst of all was the enormity of crimes committed by German leaders, adding national shame to the humiliation of defeat.

Looking for some kind of consolation, he began to read the Psalms. There he found writers expressing every sort of pain, despair, humiliation and fear. Yet running beneath these expressions of the same kinds of pain he experienced was this unquenchable sense of hope—a hope that transcended the world of wars, pain, guilt and despair.

This teen-age soldier, whose studies were interrupted by a tragic war, was drawn by this experience into reading the Bible. He returned to the university resolved to study Christian theology. Years later he wrote his monumental *Theology of Hope*, proclaiming that the central note in all Christian understanding of God was one of hope.

Hope is essential to life itself. The psychologist Viktor Frankl, in his book *From Death Camp to Existentialism*, told of his experience in a Nazi concentration camp. There, he said, he witnessed not only the horrible suffering and deaths of many men and women but also some remarkable instances of survival. Some, who lived in the same conditions, suffered the same diseases, endured the same life-threatening malnourishment and deprivation as those who died by the scores, survived the entire ordeal. "Why?" he asked. What made these survivors different?

He found that there was one common factor in these instances of survival. It was that they had something to survive *for*. It may have been a family member they wished to see again, or it might have been a project they wanted to complete. Hope has that power: it leaps beyond the circumstance of the moment. Frankl found that amid conditions where life was fragile, life was lost when hope was abandoned.

The power of hope is something we often do not understand. It comes essentially from the human tendency to transcend circumstances by virtue of the imagination. Hope, however, depends upon the fact that any set of circumstances has a larger context. Hope must be projected *outside* the circumstances.

This point is essential: hope is lost when the larger context is lost. For example, a young couple may hope to find wealth, security and fame. They hope for a beautiful, spacious home in a "good" neighborhood, money for the children's college with some to spare for vacations to Orlando, and firm possession of the top rung on the career ladder. As long as these things—whatever form they take in their imagination— remain in the realm of possibilities, they may be made quite happy by their dreams alone. After all, they have all of their lives ahead of them to realize these dreams. Or they may have many dreams and never recognize that some are contradictory and not all can be realized.

But they grow older. In middle age, it dawns on them that the capital of "time" is not quite as inexhaustible as it once seemed. Perhaps they will not realize all of their dreams. They are still in that middle-class neighborhood. Because of college expenses, they have put off vacations for several years. And changes in the career outlook over the years have made that CEO position hopelessly out-of-reach. The actual grows ever larger, ever more concrete, and the potential grows ever smaller. Hope dims because hope draws upon the power of possibility, and possibility draws from the larger contexts of life.

The truth is, therefore, that life always presents only a limited source of hope. We may project hope into future generations. Many visionaries and thinkers have imagined human aspirations fulfilled on the plane of national history or world history. Woodrow Wilson dreamed of a new world order. Machiavelli envisioned European peace. But the experience of history, unfortunately, discourages the idea that anything qualitatively different will ever occur in history—even though a few ideologies have existed on that dream. For the most part history teaches the same lesson that Koheleth, the Preacher of Ecclesiastes, learned:

> What has been will be again, what has been done will be done again;
> there is nothing new under the sun. (Eccles 1:9)

There is good reason, therefore, that hope always presupposes eternity. The limitation of hope is, in effect, the end of hope. This is why John Calvin said, "What would become of us if we did not take our stand on hope, and if our heart did not hasten beyond this world through the midst of the darkness upon the path illumined by the word and Spirit of God?"[1]

Gregory of Nyssa saw, based upon the eternity of the theological virtues, faith, hope and love, that heaven cannot simply be a state, in the sense of a final unchanging condition. Just as God is eternal, so we must always progress in hope and faith, and especially in love. What we call perfection, then, must be, not a status, but the "continued development of life to what is better." Because, St. Gregory said, "the perfection of human nature consists perhaps in its very growth in goodness."[2]

The Hopelessness of Nontranscendence

If we turn this coin on its other side we see that the loss of a sense of transcendence also necessarily means the loss of hope. In George Bernard Shaw's *Man and Superman* a remarkable passage makes reference to Dante's famous line about the inscription over the portal of hell:

> No, no, no my child: do not pray. If you do, you will throw away the main advantage of this place. Written over the gate here are the words, "Leave every hope behind, ye who enter." Only think what a relief that is! For what is hope? A form of moral responsibility. Here

there is no hope, and consequently no duty, no work, nothing to be gained by praying, nothing to be lost by doing what you like. Hell, in short, is a place where you have nothing to do but amuse yourself.[3] The idea of finally having, once and for all, what you want, what would satisfy the imagination and fulfill hope, means very much the same as abandoning hope. Hope longs for that which is not, and ceases to exist when what is hoped for is attained. It is the wellspring of work, imagination, moral responsibility. It is that which draws for us the connection between what is, what ought to be, and what might be. So the fastening of hope on temporal rewards theoretically threatens the extinction of hope because, the awful fact is, you might get what you hope for. And, then, with hope gone, only "amusement" is left.

The danger is *not*, of course, that you will satisfy every hope. The real danger is that you *think* that you will, and therefore you expend life pursuing what will never ultimately satisfy.

But why precisely does this constitute a danger? I think the loss of hope with the idea that we may realize our dreams may seem remote and unpersuasive to many people. What is more apparent, though, is an emotion that inevitably accompanies hope. However gradually and imperceptibly I have decided to "make my home" in this world, I will find beneath the surface a sense of dread and even despair. The dread comes not so much because of the prospect of death as because of the enormity of what I am proposing to do. I am proposing that if I am to find happiness, I should find it here. I think we sense there is a danger in this, because there is an almost unbearable pressure to realize the fulfillment of human desires in this life. We have the sense that we are playing with fire when we attempt to satisfy that hunger for infinite good within a world of real limits. We inevitably feel—on the community level—that the vastness of human desire for what is infinite and what is infinitely good cannot be brought into the world without destroying the world.

In this century we have had countless object lessons of how utopian dreams are turned into nightmares of despotism, enslavement, mass murder and the constant beating of war drums. On the personal level, we fear the utter disappointment of desiring that which we can imagine, knowing that the magnitude of our longing far exceeds the narrow possibilities of mortal existence.

So here is our dilemma. What does it take to make life itself satisfying? What constitutes a happy life? Philosophers from Koheleth to Camus have dealt with this problem. Invariably they have found that nothing *within* life answers to the need for satisfaction with human existence.

Koheleth, the Preacher of Ecclesiastes, examined wealth, work, pleasure and wisdom, none of which were capable of answering to the need for meaning in life. The contrast of this writing to other Old Testament writings is remarkable. People question today, as they have through the years, why such a cynical writing was included in the canon of Scripture. To many the answer seems obvious: here is a powerful statement of the futility of a life without God as the focus of human desire. It shows how futility, hopelessness and a loss of transcendence go hand in hand.

Suffering and the Crown of Life

Let's consider next how a sense of transcendence relates to the question of human suffering.

Imagine this scene. A teen-ager in third-century Alexandria stands naked at his desk, writing an urgent letter to his father. The father, a distinguished teacher of rhetoric named Leonides, has been arrested and threatened with death under Emperor Septimius Severus' policies against Christians and Jews. The son wishes only to join his father in glorious martyrdom, but his mother has spoiled his ambitions by hiding his clothes to keep him at home.

The son was Origen, later to be acknowledged as one of the greatest theologians in the history of the church. The affection between this soon-to-be-famous son and his father was well known. It was said that when the precocious Origen exasperated his father with questions about Scripture, Leonides would heartily admonish him for questions too deep for his age, and then would thank God for such a son. People also recalled how, when Origen was a small boy, Leonides would stand gazing in admiration at his sleeping son. Then, baring the small boy's chest, he would reverently kiss it as "a shrine consecrated by the divine spirit."[4]

Writing this letter, the young man poured forth his affection for his father; yet the form it took is not as we would expect. It did not focus anxiously on the prospect of never seeing his father again, nor did it betray a concern that the family's prosperity was sure to be confiscated, leaving them destitute. Instead he fears that his father might weaken out of tender consideration for the family. "Take heed," he writes his beloved father, "not to change thy mind on account of us."[5] He pleads not for earthly safety but for his father's eternal glory.

We cannot help, in our age of very different habits of the heart, being astonished at young Origen's turn of mind. Something of the atmosphere of the early Christian community must have made such sentiments plausible, whereas they are quite difficult to imagine today. Even the mode in which these kinds of events were reported a few decades later strike us as expressions from a very different world than ours. For instance, when Eusebius writes of Plutarch, Origen's martyred student, he does not say Plutarch was "tortured pitilessly to death" (which he was) but that he was "crowned with divine martyrdom."[6] The brother of Plutarch, Heraclas, thinking nothing of the danger, would accompany Christians to their trial, stand by them with encouraging and cheerful words as they were led to execution, and in the face of a hostile, rock-throwing crowd "with great freedom salute the brethren with a kiss," all the more infuriating the enemies of Christ.

The church did not always produce martyrs, of course. There were those also who fell away from the faith, intimidated by the ghastly prospects of cruel public spectacles and anxious over family misfortunes. But the overwhelming tide of boldness that carried the church along in those days is undeniable. Stories from all over the Mediterranean bear the note of heroism in suffering and of fellowship and joy in the pains of martyrdom, to a degree not found in any other movement in history.

Commenting on a largely Christianized society of one century later,

Charles Kingsley caught the spirit of the fruits of this movement when he wrote that Christ "had awakened in the heart of mankind a moral craving never before felt in any strength, except by a few isolated philosophers and prophets . . . and from one end of the Empire to the other, from the slave in the mill to the emperor on his throne, all hearts were either hungering and thirsting after righteousness, or learning to do homage to those who did so."[7]

Yet it is important to see that these Christians were never motivated by thoughts of the temporal improvement of society. Whether Christianity itself would improve society or whether contemporary institutions were beyond redemption was a matter of some dispute as well as much indifference. But they all agreed that, whether or not the world improved, their sacrifices were devoted to an entirely different order of being. It was a suffering endured for the sake of a transcendent glory.

They would remember the words of the apostle Paul that "our present sufferings are not worth comparing with the glory that will be revealed in us" (Rom 8:18). In the account of a certain Blandina's torture, for instance, among many other similar accounts, one feels drawn into the sympathies of another time and place—one with radically transcendent values:

> Blandina . . . was bound and suspended on a stake, and thus exposed as food to the assaults of wild beasts, and as she thus appeared to hang after the manner of the cross, by her earnest prayers she infused much alacrity into the contending martyrs. For as they saw her in the contest . . . they contemplated Him that was crucified for them, to persuade those that believe in Him, that every one who suffers for Christ, will for ever enjoy communion with the loving God.[8]

The persecuted church presented a thoroughgoing idea that every earthly expectation was subservient to the eternal object of life. A Christian apologist from the middle of the second century, giving typical expression to this idea, said, "They live in their own home-towns, but only as sojourners; they bear their share in all things as citizens, but endure all hardships as foreigners. Every foreign land is home to them, and every home is foreign. . . . Their existence is on earth, but their citizenship is in heaven. . . . They love all, and are persecuted by all. "9 We can hardly understand the strength of this persecuted church to spread its message and to transform the Roman world without seeing the radical nature of its devotion to eternal concerns.

Suffering and the Ideal Life

Now think of the contrast between *that* vision of life and the one commonly found today, especially as we relate to the question of suffering. The problem that arises in a view of the world that is tacitly closed to any transcendent reality is that if suffering occurs it must be resolved in this life. That means it must be (1) justified by the conviction that everyone gets what he or she deserves, (2) justified on the basis of some compensation within life or (3) denied as unreal and illusory. Those three responses are nontranscendent *religious* options, as well as explanations within a secular world view. However, within a secular world, they seem to work best when a society is wealthy enough to insulate people from life's manifold pains and tragedies for at least part of their lives. And hope being the almost inextinguishable human emotion, people in a secular culture continue to assert that things will finally "work out" and that one must be "optimistic."

Richard Weaver, observing this tendency in an increasingly secular American society, called it a "hysterical optimism." A society that has denied transcendence cannot bear the thought that there will not be a resolution of suffering in this life. Yet everywhere is the evidence that pain is unequal and widespread, and ends not in some resolution that makes us happy and content, but in fact ends in death. Ironically, the "hysterical optimism" of secular culture may take the form of religion. (We will deal with this point in a later chapter.) But, in any event, it expects—and, in fact, the reality of suffering demands—that happiness be attained in this life.

The need to resolve suffering and guarantee happiness in this life is so subtly intrusive into every area of life that we hardly notice that it has invaded even the church. But it is important to note that this response can't help but seem alien to the Christian gospel, or we might have to say that the Christian gospel seems quite alien to the dream of temporal relief from suffering.

The classical Christian attitude toward suffering is not only *one* of the features of Christianity, it is the central thought of Christianity from the very beginning. The cross was its symbol precisely because it represented shame, suffering and injustice that is resolved in the resurrection of the dead. The vigorous transcendent expectations of Christianity meant that it had the power to take the suffering of life into the very heart of its thinking and devotion.

Simone Weil centered much of her thought upon this Christian insight. "The extreme greatness of Christianity," she said, "lies in the fact that it does not seek a supernatural remedy for suffering, but a supernatural use for it."[10] The idea that suffering should somehow be resolved in this life takes the very heart out of this Christian insight.

"That Hideous Strength"

The strength of the urge toward heaven cannot be denied. It is why the world at large—and we can include the East as well as the West in this—had always suspected that just the reverse of secularism is really true: this world is *not* our home.

Whether we turn to Hinduism, with its many forms of world-denying asceticism, or to Taoism with its confidence that the "Way" of life is a "divine Principle which informs and underlies nature"[11] and thus lies beyond the known world, we see this same intuition that in this world we are strangers and sojourners. The ways in which this denial of the world is expressed are many. Orthodox Christianity will interpret the "foreignness" of the world quite distinctly. In Hinduism, for instance, intuition about our homelessness in the world argues that the sensible world is *maya*, or illusion. In Zoroastrianism the same insight results in a dualism of good and evil to explain our tension with the world. Closer to Christianity is the Taoist view of a transcendent "way" that incorporates the world, or the idea of ancient Greeks, beginning with Heraclitus, that a logos penetrates every aspect of existence. They believed in a principle, a "Word," that ordered the world from outside the world. Christianity adopted the logos idea, of course, to explain their own doctrine of the transcendent God who was both over the world and incarnate in the world.

More than religious doctrine, however, a certain practice that extends over all the world of faith confirms this observation. Every religious faith, to some degree and in different ways, expresses itself in ascetic practices. That is, it engages in a world-denying discipline of the appetites or the senses, such as fasting, voluntary poverty, chastity, living apart from society, and so on. Here we see from every part of the globe a huge concerted effort of humanity to deal with the tensions of living in a world to which it feels it does not fully belong.

Some people will object that asceticism is abnormal and sometimes pathological. We would have to respond that something that widespread, throughout the world and throughout history, might still not be called universally popular, but could hardly be called abnormal. And the extent to which it has at times become pathological only emphasizes that the anxiety of humanity's tension with the world is a great one. For there is nowhere that reason and moderation are not regularly disregarded in an effort to confront the anxiety of our inescapable sense of foreignness in the world.

We might conclude, along with certain cynics, of course, that the whole human race is mad. Or we might more reasonably assume that a great truth lies behind this universal suspicion that the world we sense is not, by itself, the world for which we are made.

The same idea is so strongly suggested in the Bible that you cannot understand the Bible without it.

The psalmist, for instance, speaks of his foolish envy toward those who prosper in their evil ways in Psalm 73. In a remarkable poem he leads us to understand his bitterness and then his enlightenment to the fact that what he envies pales into insignificance before the real aim of

life. "When my heart was grieved and my spirit embittered, I was sense-
less and ignorant; I was a brute beast before you" (vv. 21-22). He finally
discovers that life is not aimed at these trifles that his contemporaries
strive for because afterward he will be received in glory:

> Whom have I in heaven but you? And being with you, I desire noth-
> ing on earth. My flesh and my heart may fail, but God is the strength
> of my heart and my portion forever. (vv. 25-26)

Paul speaks of earthly life as continual awareness of the incompleteness
of life, and of the awkwardness of our present existence. Now we live
in a *tent;* God has, however, prepared for us a *house:*

> Now we know that if the earthly tent we live in is destroyed, we have
> a building from God, an eternal house in heaven, not built by human
> hands. Meanwhile we groan, longing to be clothed with our heavenly
> dwelling. . . . For while we are in this tent, we groan and are bur-
> dened, because we do not wish to be unclothed, but to be clothed
> with our heavenly dwelling, so that what is mortal may be swallowed
> up by life. (2 Cor 5:1-4)

From Paul's point of view, or from the psalmist's point of view, we can
understand and even accept the strangeness of our situation. We have
anxiety in this world, but we should expect to because we are not made
for the narrowness of mortality. The mortality, Paul says in this won-
derfully apt image, will be swallowed up in life (that is, not done away
with, but become complete). Thus the circumstances of this life always
stand under the judgment of eternity. This means that they are not
superseded and made insignificant by the glory to come. Instead, in the
life of eternal glory their true meaning and importance come to light and
are even magnified!

When I have decided, however, that this world is *indeed* my home, then
that same anxiety which is thrust upon the incompleteness of this life
results in a very different attitude. This world is not the way it is
supposed to be. Or, if it is, then there is something wrong with me.

If I assume the first, I may become a revolutionary. I am trying to
make the world fit an ideal. Or my ideals have caused me simply to reject

the world as it is. Perhaps it must be burned down, shattered to the core, so that an ideal world will arise in its place.

This is an attempt to make the world my home, to change circumstances, thus resolving the anxiety that Paul refers to, and that every great soul senses as the central ground of the human experience. It is one way of trying to solve the dilemma.

The other way is to accommodate myself to the world I find. I assume that I am poorly adjusted. The answer is, for instance, psychoanalysis. Or the answer is finding a key to the system that will make me comfortable, successful and happy—that is, something that will make me at home in the world. At all costs I do not want to be a stranger in the world, for the world is my home.

This *domestication of the world* is the urge that we find behind what we call secularism. It is not secularism per se that differs with the central thrust of Christianity. But it is this persistent aim to resolve the pain of life, either through changing the outward world or through a personal accommodation to the world, that strikes directly against the core of a Christian view of life.

On a large scale, people in the United States have experienced both of these over a span of two decades. In the sixties people attempted to "change the world" through revolution and social restructuring. The prophets of this age argued that basic problems in society reflected errors in the "structures of society." By the eighties there had been a decided reaction against the revolutionary culture, and eventually what seemed to be a wholesale adoption of middle-class values proved to be an attempt to make the world work for us (or "for me"). Magazines aimed at this culture were increasingly unapologetically self-centered: the earlier titles of *Life* and *People* gave way to *Us*, then *Self*. In both cases—in revolution or accommodation—what began with hope ended in despair. The social and political hopes of the sixties turned to gruesome dreams of world-denying cultures in the Manson murders and the Jonestown suicides. The sane and safe self-centeredness of yuppie greed in the eighties revealed its inner depravity in Wall Street and Washington scandals and a country awash with drug traffic at all levels of society, devastating the ambitious, young middle class.

These are merely the externals, the superstructure that attaches itself to a strange and profound irony. It is inevitably the case that when we declare this world our home, when we protest against the abstractions of heaven and when we concern ourselves with the concreteness of this life, we actually find ourselves more estranged than ever from the world. When we are most intent on living in this world—as if it were the full extent of reality—we find ourselves most dissatisfied. We think not of the world itself but of how it might be changed or how it might be used. The world is clouded over with notions of a more or less pragmatic nature. And what we actually see (and therefore *live with*) is not at all the real world, but our ambitions for it, our wishes to use it toward some unfulfilled end, or our notions of some ideal world that never did, nor ever shall, exist.

In our attempt to overcome estrangement and to make for ourselves a home of the world, we have made ourselves, more than ever, strangers.

The two primary questions of life—What can we hope for? and Why do we suffer?—are both addressed on a different level in the question of self-transcendence. It is a question that can only be adequately posed by asking "Who am I?" That is the third and most significant question that the Christian concept of heaven addresses. It is also a question that gives us a clue to an inescapable frustration in a society that has lost its sense of heaven. We will explore this question in the following chapter.

CHAPTER 5

SELF-
TRANSCENDENCE

Keep on loving each other as brothers.
Do not forget to entertain strangers, for by
so doing some people have entertained angels
without knowing it.

Hebrews 13:1-2

•　•　•

"THERE WAS A MAN WHO HAD TWO SONS," JESUS BEGAN (LK 15:11). THE YOUNGER
son took his inheritance and journeyed into a far country where he
wasted his fortune.

Now, for the parable to make sense we have to assume that for as
long as the money lasted, the prodigal son felt quite at home in the far
country. It wasn't until the cash gave out and the country was in famine
and he found himself feeding the swine, all the while sorely tempted to
eat along with them, that he "came to himself" (v. 17 RSV), as the text
says.

Like an alarm, the thought penetrated the fog of his habitual far-
country living: *he was not really at home!* At that moment nothing had
changed regarding his condition, but everything had changed in his
relationship to it. He "came to himself" when the far country was no

longer home, and he remembered his father and his true home. In the sudden shock of discovering the strangeness of his circumstances, in his suddenly feeling no longer at home, he discovered the truth about himself. And the truth came all in a rush as he reflected upon the distance he had placed between himself and the home he left behind.

It is worth noting, however, that until then the prodigal stubbornly clung to the hope of making a home where he was, even to the point of taking meals with a swineherd, which would have been extremely degrading to a Jew. Adaptation, after all, is second nature—and we will pursue it sometimes with every inventive power at hand.

A few years ago I visited an American family living in the beautiful Chinese port city of Chilung. Outside this home the sights and sounds of the Orient were everywhere. But inside I was immediately struck by the familiarity of my surroundings. An Andrew Wyeth painting hung over a couch that I judged to be of the "Thomasville" make, distinctly American. Thrown over a wooden rocker was a quilt, such as you might associate with Appalachia. I could easily imagine I was in Chicago or Atlanta. I talked with this family about their American-style living habits. The tendency persists everywhere: we adapt to our strange surroundings by making them somehow familiar, by blunting their strangeness. We domesticate our foreign world.

Mircea Eliade describes how numerous ancient peoples constructed their homes by first driving a large stake into the ground or fixing a central pillar. This point they identified as the center, or "navel," of the world. And in building their houses they located the *axis mundi*, so that their home became a miniature cosmos: it organized the world for them, making them sense that they were at home in the world. It makes no difference that their neighbors did the same thing and that *their* homes also were founded on the "center of the world." The point is that the symbol itself gives them a way of being oriented and at home in an otherwise strange world that always resists being domesticated, comfortable and predictable.[1]

It is the way of making a home into a small cosmos; but it is also a way of making the cosmos a home.

When the apostle Paul wrote to Philippian Christians he was aware of how important their principle of re-creating a home in a foreign place was for them. Philippi was a colony of Rome—a part of the Roman commonwealth. This meant more than its being a subject city: Philippi was distinct from other cities in Macedonia in that it was made to be a model Roman city. In a colony one would find Roman customs, Roman architecture, Roman dress, and the prevailing language was Latin. It was, in a word, a fragment of Rome. If you were to walk into the city, you would have the feeling of entering an Italian suburb of Rome, even though it was nearly a thousand miles distant. So, when Paul was writing those Philippian Christians, he knew they would understand him when he said, "Our commonwealth is in heaven" (Phil 3:20 RSV).

But there is an important difference between Paul's calling Christians to be citizens of a heavenly commonwealth and the human tendency to make a home on foreign soil by imitating the customs of the homeland. The difference is simply that no matter how courageous and inventive our efforts, we Christians must never forget that this world is not home. There is a sense of alienation that must be taken into the heart of all experiences. Adaptation may be second nature, but it can also be the death of our first nature—that created in the image of God and then re-created by the grace of God in Christ.

This same admonition, probably the most frequent of the apostolic teachings, is repeated in every segment of the New Testament. While this sense of alienation enters into religious sentiments of all religions, what distinguishes the New Testament is that its writers *do not wish to resolve that sense of alienation*. Rather, they want to know it fully and to preserve it as the very key to life's secret.

Note the following from every separate classification of New Testament writings:

☐ *The Synoptic Gospels:*

"If anyone would come after me, he must deny himself and take up his cross and follow me. For whoever wants to save his life will lose it, but whoever loses his life for me and for the gospel will save it. What good is it for a man to gain the whole world, yet forfeit his soul?" (Mk 8:34-36).

☐ *The Gospel of John:*

"If the world hates you, keep in mind that it hated me first. If you belonged to the world, it would love you as its own. As it is, you do not belong to the world, but I have chosen you out of the world. That is why the world hates you" (Jn 15:18-19).

☐ *Pauline Epistles:*

"Do not conform any longer to the pattern of this world, but be transformed by the renewing of your mind. Then you will be able to test and approve what God's will is—his good, pleasing and perfect will" (Rom 12:2).

"If only for this life we have hope in Christ, we are to be pitied more than all men" (1 Cor 15:19).

"For our light and momentary troubles are achieving for us an eternal glory that far outweighs them all. So we fix our eyes not on what is seen, but on what is unseen. For what is seen is temporary, but what is unseen is eternal" (2 Cor 4:17-18).

"But whatever was to my profit I now consider loss for the sake of Christ. What is more, I consider everything a loss compared to the surpassing greatness of knowing Christ Jesus my Lord, for whose sake I have lost all things. I consider them rubbish, that I may gain Christ" (Phil 3:7-8).

"Since, then, you have been raised with Christ, set your hearts on things above, where Christ is seated at the right hand of God. Set your minds on things above, not on earthly things" (Col 3:1-2).

"For Demas, because he loved this world, has deserted me. . . . But the Lord stood at my side and gave me strength . . . and will bring me safely to his heavenly kingdom" (2 Tim 4:10, 17-18).

☐ *General Epistles:*

"Dear friends, I urge you, as aliens and strangers in the world, to abstain from sinful desires, which war against your soul" (1 Pet 2:11).

"Do not love the world or anything in the world. If anyone loves the world, the love of the Father is not in him. For everything in the world—the cravings of sinful man, the lust of his eyes and the boasting of what he does—comes not from the Father but from the world. The world and its desires pass away, but the man who does the will of God lives forever" (1 Jn 2:15-17).

□ *Revelation:*

(To the church in Laodicea): "You say, 'I am rich; I have acquired wealth and do not need a thing.' But you do not realize that you are wretched, pitiful, poor, blind and naked" (Rev 3:17).

I have mentioned only a small selection of passages here with no real effort to be systematic or complete. It's enough merely to suggest the thoroughness with which the New Testament is anchored in the proposition that the aim of life is altogether outside of life. For in every part of the canon we find these consistent and urgent warnings to New Testament Christians against making a home in this world.

Why were New Testament writers so consistently opposed to Christians' accommodating themselves to the world? Where was the threat? What did they see in the notion of being "at home in this world" that was so disastrous to the faith? I will try to demonstrate what I believe to be the answer to this question: it is that forgetting heaven not only loses the fully sufficient hope that the anticipation of heaven provides, and loses sight of the problem of suffering that the hope of heaven addresses—both of which we dealt with in the previous chapter—but also fails to address a centrally important human requirement. The very center of Christianity and the very real effect of a desire for heaven is the call to self-transcendence. It is, in fact, the call to awaken to grace—to love. And this call or vocation is conceived in New Testament thought as the true discovery of one's self: for "whoever loses his life for my sake will find it" (Mt 10:39).

Heaven and Self-Transcendence

In his editorial column in the *Christian Index*, Al Mohler has frequently shed light on the growing self-centeredness of modern life—a preoccupation that he has found in the church as well as outside the church. He wrote about it again in a recent editorial:

> Those who doubt the self-movement in the church need look no further than your local Christian book store or church library. Sociologist James Davison Hunter recently surveyed the products of the six largest evangelical publishing houses. He discovered that fully 87.5 percent of all books released from those publishers concerned self-help issues. That means that only 12.5 percent of all books from those *evangelical* publishers were books on theology, doctrine, ethical issues, biblical commentary and other central concerns. The therapeutic has triumphed even in the household of faith.

Then Mohler goes on to cite a *Newsweek* cover story on the great new surge of interest in the church. But the attraction of the church has taken on a new character. The greatest crowds arrive, says the article, at midweek, and "instead of filing into the pews, these people head for the basement, where they immediately sit down and begin talking about their deepest secrets, darkest fears and strangest cravings."[2]

This observation by Albert Mohler and the writers at *Newsweek* sets in relief the principal effect that the longing for heaven has had upon the church. That is, heaven, more than anything else means self-transcendence. The reality of a heaven, for which this world exists, is self-transcendence on the cosmic level. And heaven as the real destiny of the human soul means self-transcendence on the personal level. It signifies that life is not complete here, and therefore will not find its fulfillment in this world. The center of life is outside our personal experience: it finds its center in God, not in the individual or in the world itself.

This means that the whole structure of being, for those who seek heaven, implies a reaching out, or a reaching forward, to that which is outside the self. It is the realization that life is not essentially self-expression, but grace; it is dependent upon and focuses upon that which is beyond and outside. The secret enshrined in the Christian vision of heaven is that life can only be expended (because it is lived for an other);

it cannot be saved or saved up, it cannot be protected or mastered. It can only be given.

The Collapsed Boundaries of Self and World

What is the meaning of this experience I am calling "the domestication of the world"? The phrase is not a conventional one in philosophy or theology. But I think it might prove useful. It corresponds to something we all know.

Once I put the issue to some students this way: "Have you ever noticed that when you move into a new house or a new apartment it seems like an alien environment? You're not quite 'at home' until things become familiar. And little by little you grow accustomed to the colors, the furnishings, the neighborhood."

These students, like most, are fairly mobile. They've had the personal experience, usually quite recent, of moving into a new dorm room or a new apartment, and they knew what I was saying. Michael, a senior, volunteered, "It doesn't look right, it doesn't smell right, it doesn't feel right."

"Exactly! It feels like an alien environment. But that feeling does not last: in some circumstances it might last longer than others, but in a matter of days, the sharp sense of being out of place in these new surroundings subsides. But for that brief time you notice things in a different way—you notice their strangeness. They have not yet been absorbed into your world. More than likely you do not react strongly to this sensation. But it plays upon your mind and imagination: the design and color of the wallpaper, the peculiar angle of the doorstop, the broken concrete on the patio."

Linda, who at first looked skeptical, finally began to nod in agreement. She didn't know, she said, that other people felt that way about new places and thought she was just a bit peculiar in her feeling about the strangeness of things. "It takes some time," she said, "but then I begin to feel that psychologically I have moved in."

"And when does that happen?"

"Oh, after I get the bed in the right place . . . and the desk . . . and the TV . . . and after I can find the bathroom in the dark!"

"So, some things you change, and other things you get accustomed to."

"That's right. I don't know when it happens, but it's like one day I'm a visitor in this strange room . . . and I'm living with 'other people's stuff' all around me. And the next day, it's just me. It's my place, and it doesn't seem strange anymore."

The other students laughed, but you could tell it was not just out of their good humor or Linda's comic expression. They were laughing, as we often do, out of the surprise of *recognition*. Mark said it happened to him as soon as he spread out the old familiar Clemson Tiger rug—then he was at home.

"It would take a 'Georgia Bulldog Rug' for me," Mark's companion jibed. But he and the rest agreed that the time comes when you've adjusted.

"When does it happen?" I asked, pressing them for some kind of awareness of what made them finally feel at home. When, I was asking, does the strangeness disappear?

"It's when you no longer notice," Linda said. I could tell, however, that she wasn't quite satisfied with her own answer. She turned toward the large vertical window in the lecture room. Almost as if she *saw* the answer outside, she turned her face toward me again.

"You notice, I guess—you *do* notice," she said, "but it's different."

"How different?" I asked, having no idea where we were heading.

"It's like this: at first you see something you've never seen before. Even though you see it several times, you're still noticing it. But the time comes when you don't just see it, but you also *remember* it."

"I think the feeling," Mark added, "is that the thing you see has become a part of you."

"It's like that magnolia tree outside this window," Linda continued. "I've seen it a thousand times, but most of the time I don't notice it because I think I've already seen it. I'm just remembering it."

Our conversation went on in this vein. The once-strange features in a new environment become familiar items centered in our life, no longer alien from us but a part of us. In other words, domestication means breaking down the uncomfortable barrier of strangeness and, at the same time, no longer seeing these things as something *given into* life, but taking them for granted. They have become more or less extensions of our selves.

Significantly, Tony remarked that when you are in a new place, there is a certain something, "you could call it luster," a certain awe of things, that is lost after a while.

"Things lose their 'luster'?" I asked.

"Yes."

"And do people?"

"I suppose so," he said.

Quickly we moved to the subject of personal relations. I recalled the lines from *Our Town* where Emily Webb is allowed to enter back into life—having died fourteen years earlier—and spend a day at home, on her twelfth birthday. Thorton Wilder uses this device to make us powerfully aware of our losing touch with people, even people we love, in a habitual familiarity with life.

Emily is filled with wonder as she sees her parents in the kitchen. ("They're so young and beautiful.") Later, with her mother she appeals urgently:

Oh, Mama, just look at me one minute as though you really saw me. Mama, fourteen years have gone by. I'm dead. . . . But, just for a moment now we're all together. Mama, just for a moment we're happy. *Let's look at one another.* (act 3)

If a sense of transcendence is when we "look at one another," attend to that outside ourselves, then we begin to see what are the marks of nontranscendence.

Nontranscendence is self-absorption. As such it expresses itself in three ways: as isolation, as appetite and as death. Let's look briefly at each of these manifestations of nontranscendence.

Nontranscendence as Isolation

This conversation with students revealed a paradox in our everyday experience. We desire intimacy; there is a longing to feel "at home" with people and things and to come to know a setting. At the same time, however, that means losing some of the sharpness of distinction between "myself" and "the other." The extreme of familiarity is when no "other" answers to my "self," no "absolute" answers to my "relative." A thoroughly intimate world is, in other words, a world of broken barriers, where the boundary between self and other has virtually collapsed. The other extreme, however, would be a world of sharp distinctions. It would be a fragmented world, one without a sense of unity and without fellowship—a world of strangers.

In a world that lacks a sense of transcendence, however, it is obviously the fragmentation that troubles us most. We tend to see distinction itself as a threat. Unity, without a transcendent point of reference, can only be bought at the price of sacrificing distinction. In essence, the less we believe in God the more we are threatened by distinctions. In humanity, for instance, unity is threatened by the distinctions of race and sex. In a world with a healthy belief in transcendent reality, it is possible to think of our unity in relation to God. Distinction does not diminish that unity: it is a unity of fellowship and community in which distinctions can even enhance unity.

However, in a nontranscendent world the search for unity requires more radical adjustments. If unity, purpose and meaning are to be found within the world then distinction can only be seen as a problem—it is evidence of alienation and is experienced as pain. Therefore, a nontranscendent world tends to "solve" this dilemma in one of two ways. One is by saying that the distinction is, in fact, not real. In an effort to be "at home in the world," distinction is refused a place in philosophical calculations of what really counts in the world. The other way is by withdrawing into individualistic isolation and seeing the pain of distinction as a signal that the world must be made to conform to the desires of the isolated self.

Mother love can become "smother love"; a father can want to realize his own ambitions through a son. Examples abound of one person's losing a sense of the distinction (and therefore not honoring the distinction) between the self and another person. In this hatred of distinction—of that which would dare be independent of me—we see the heart of evil. This temptation to see another as only an object in one's own world, as an extension of the ego, is always present in relationships. Hitler could devastate the German nation only because he identified its future absolutely with his own. It is not accidental that the Bible envisions Satan as he who goes to and fro on the earth seeking whom he may devour. Evil almost always has as its object the devouring of that which is separate to make it a part of the empire of self.

By contrast a world that believes in heaven is a world that envisions that the structure of personal reality involves division, alienation and distinction. One grows and matures through this problem, but one does not utterly solve it. We live in the far country, but our home is elsewhere. We belong to that home country all the more strongly because we feel the pain of separation and have not forgotten. For one who believes in heaven, happiness cannot be the kind of forgetfulness in which we merely submerge our desires for what the far country offers. It would be feeding on the pods that the swine ate—a form of misery. Better to endure the pain of separation, knowing that happiness may be included in this world but can never be captured in this world.

Nontranscendence as Appetite

The great gulf that divides a transcendent from a nontranscendent sense of reality appears in the *interpretation* of this desire for intimacy and the fact of separation. It is an interpretation that takes place at every level of the personality—emotional, intellectual and volitional.

The nontranscendent impulse desires to overcome its separateness from the world of things and people, from reality, directly. It looks toward the dissolution of distinction, especially the distinction between the self and outside reality. That otherness is seen as a barrier. The nontranscendent impulse is ultimately self-centered. If things and people do not center in the self—that is, if they exist as alien from the self—then they threaten to perpetuate the self in its own feelings of isolation and estrangement. To domesticate one's world is to center the world in one's self. It is to overcome the barrier of otherness.

The transcendent grounding of human experience, however, senses that the "otherness" of things, of people and of reality at large is the clue to the essential meaning of life. The self is not bound to include reality into its small circle of existence, but is free to find a way out into the world. For it is in this intractable "otherness" of reality that one is free to love, to rise above self-interests. George MacDonald said once that another human being is the "doorway out of the prison of self." Nontranscendence means nothing less than perpetual isolation, while transcendence recognizes a "beyond" that begins at the doorway of otherness. A sense of the transcendent recognizes—and means nothing without this recognition—that pain cannot be extinguished by enclosing the world in one's self. Rather, it knows that pain is the means by which to give oneself. Asked to choose between a great unknowable, uncontrollable, but real world to live in, and a world that one has the comfort of knowing intimately—a controllable world, a comfortable world, a world militant against suffering, but a world of narrow possibilities and an unreal world—a person with a sense of transcendence recognizes the greater, more dangerous, real world.

Nontranscendence as Death

All this may seem no more than to repeat the cliché "No matter how wealthy (or famous, or successful, or popular) you become, it won't make you happy." You sense that this is true, though you don't know why. But when you *say* what you want in unguarded moments, you'll still say you want more money, more prestige, more friends and so on. And in a world that has lost its former expressions of transcendence, there is nothing to remind you that this isn't the way, that it's a dead end. Common wisdom seems to confirm only your first impulse, not your deeper sense of what satisfies. "You only go round once," the voices say. "Go for it."

The language of nontranscendence is the language of possession, conquest, appropriation, ambition; it is the language of the devouring, insatiable, imperial ego. It is the ego that can be wounded, resentful and disappointed because, measuring its misery by the comparable success of someone who has more, does more, is more noticed and more praised, it cannot been satisfied. It is the ego that enjoys its moment of triumph and the misery of its rivals. It is an ego with the most fragile hold upon the joys of life, knowing the next moment might bring misery by the discovery of that which it does not yet have or cannot have. It is an ego whose identity is increasingly a borrowed thing, dependent upon that part of the outside world it would hope to gain. And it is an ego that sooner or later realizes the absolute limit that reality places upon any possession and, therefore, on any hopes. Time finally robs the ego of even its greatest conquests and its fondest hopes. "What good will it be for a man if he gains the whole world, yet forfeits his soul?"

But the heart of nontranscendence, with its language of possession, power and prestige, is that it seeks to simplify the world. It seeks to transform the world into a new solar system with itself as the sun. And in so doing it seeks to divest the world of its other things, other persons, other interests, other powers. In short, it dissolves the complexity and the interrelatedness of the world, turning it into a compact dwelling. The only problem is that the dwelling turns out to be not so large as the soul imagined. Ultimately it excludes the world and contains only the one who would possess it. Strangely, it is a world not suited to live in; it is not large enough. But if we were to think of this dwelling in terms of its size, we need not imagine it any larger than a coffin.

Transcendence and Otherness

I am reminded of Queequeg's coffin in *Moby Dick* when I think of this comparison between a tamed, reduced, domesticated world and a box for burial. Queequeg had arranged for his own coffin to be made, properly appointed with a spearhead, a flask of water and so on. He had himself placed in the coffin and was ready to die.

But one thing saved him. He thought of some duty left undone on shore. So he rose up and refused to die just yet. It was that which transcended him that gave him a reason to live.

Thus is it always. Life arises from relationship and the sense of otherness. Death is the resolution of all that contradicts self because it is the end of relationship.

The real meaning of transcendence is captured in the apostle Paul's listing of those qualities he called the fruits of the Spirit: love, joy, peace, patience, kindness, goodness, faithfulness, gentleness, self-control. Each one is marked by circumscribing the limits of self and becoming aware of the other.

The result of these fruits of the Spirit are personal qualities that hinge on relationship. Two that would immediately occur to us—and whose presence or absence make all the difference in personal character—are sympathy and humor. When these are present we find also the quality of being unburdened by self-centeredness, and a genuine interest in that which lies quite outside self-interest.

Sympathy, for instance, is the quality of entering into others' experience. It is more than feeling their pain; it is attending to them, whether emotionally, intellectually or otherwise. It is the ability to be detached from matters of self-interest, opinions and personal prejudices and to be engaged by the mind and spirit of another person.

I learned a valuable lesson from a professor of mine during graduate studies. Professor David Mueller, whose expertise embraces such widely disparate theologies as Albrecht Ritschl's liberalism and Karl Barth's neo-orthodoxy, had assigned me a reading of a theologian whose views I, from the very beginning, detested. In my conversation with him, I brought out all my best efforts at a critique of the theologian.

"Did you read this theologian?" Dr. Mueller asked.

I was more than a little taken off-guard by his question. "Yes, of course." And I had, in fact, read his work very carefully—all the time looking for the fallacies, searching for the fatal flaws that discredited his approach and thus justified my own theology.

"No," Mueller said, "I mean did you really want to know what he was thinking? Because you really have to read someone sympathetically before you can say you've read them. First, assume you can learn something from this person. Sit at his feet for a while. Listen carefully. Then once you understand, you are qualified to launch your critique."

This comment turned out to be an important part of my education, and I have tried to pass the attitude on to my students. But the lesson actually applies to more than theology. The honesty and helpfulness of judgment—of anything, whether of art, literature, personal behavior—must first at least attempt to free itself of self-centeredness and self-interest. To the degree that it becomes *sympathetic*, it gains the power to be truthful.

This sense of otherness or detachment is seen not only in sympathy but in the closely related quality of humor. Humor requires detachment—that is, not detachment from others but detachment from the superstition of self-importance. Being a god, after all, is too serious a matter to leave room for laughter. G. K. Chesterton said, "Angels can fly because they take themselves lightly."

I was reminded of that Chestertonian quip while spending an afternoon with Martha Franks, a retired missionary to China who spent forty years there and then returned to South Carolina and with undiminished energy founded a Christian retirement home. With Miss Franks on my arm, my wife and I were being escorted around the large establishment she had inspired and built.

Here was a woman of advanced age and great beauty whose most notable characteristic was her self-effacing sense of humor. She knew the day was coming when she would have to move out of her house to the more secure dormitory-like home. Taking no thought of playing the part of a saint (which is why I know she is one), she said she'd just rather not live with someone else. She never had to, being unmarried all these years, and she didn't want to now.

"It's not that I'm afraid of my roommate being ornery," she said. "You could handle that."

"Then what is it?" I asked, playing along.

"The real problem is if they turn out to be nice. Then you have to be nice all the time, and that's a strain."

Humor like Martha Frank's is almost a precondition of virtue. Self-absorption is not only the death of virtue, it is also the end of humor. That leads me to think (and this will be my only speculative statement about heaven) that in heaven there is plenty of laughter ("The One enthroned in heaven laughs; the Lord scoffs at them," Ps 2:4). Humor, like sympathy, is almost synonymous with a transcendent point of reference.

There is a kind of humor that does not fit this description, but it is almost always either cruel or despairing. It sees the nonsensical elements in life, but it views these things from the standpoint of power and omniscience, like a healthy young man laughing at the handicapped or the brilliant student amused at the struggles of a less-gifted classmate. Humor based upon cruelty, violence or sarcasm must maintain the fiction of a self-centered world. I think it is an important question (though perhaps more than we can take up here) whether the humor of contemporary mass media and film is not increasingly of this nontranscendent variety.

But this exception merely underlines the fact that there is a humor and a sympathy that build upon relationship and become impossible without it. What is widely recognized is that the quality we most long for in people are these very ones—humor and sympathy. Does that not give us a clue that something most essential to the human spirit is found there? And perhaps it is here in this enormous attraction of self-transcendence, our attraction to people who can, so to speak, "get outside of themselves," that we find ready evidence of Jesus' promise that "whoever loses his life for me and for the gospel will save it" (Mk 8:35).

CHAPTER 6

COMMUNITY AS HUMAN RESOURCE

You know as well as we do that in human
discussion justice enters only where the
pressure of necessity is equal. For the rest,
the powerful exact what they can and the
weak grant what they must.

Thucydides, *Syngraphe*

You trample on the poor and force him to give
you grain. Therefore, though you have built
stone mansions, you will not live in them.

Amos 5:11

•   •   •

A PIECE OUT OF ALICE IN WONDERLAND *REMINDS ME OF THE DILEMMA WE FACE*
in a world that still yearns for something but no longer remembers quite
what it is.

Alice meets the Cheshire-Cat and anxiously asks:

"Would you tell me, please, which way I ought to go from here?"

"That depends a good deal on where you want to get to," said
the Cat.

"I don't much care where—" said Alice. "Then it doesn't matter
which way you go," said the Cat.[1]
In the practical results of losing our transcendent purpose, we find the
clashing of two contradictory conditions. Like Alice we have intense
desires and confused aims. This can be seen in every area of life. We
seem to be working inexorably to bring about moral confusion, cultural
darkness and egotistical ruthlessness. There are three areas where what
is basically a confusion of relationship can be seen. The first is in the
relationships within society, where men and women, having lost their
eternal destiny, now become objects within the world and "resources"
for purposes that are now nontranscendent and pragmatic. The second
area is in human relationships to the natural order, which is now defined
by nontranscendent purposes and is thus subject to scientific and technological designs. And the third is in the area of religion, where the
"supernatural" is increasingly viewed as the means toward a nontranscendent purpose, producing a peculiar fanaticism and obsession in religious quests.

In this chapter and the following three I want to suggest what is the
nature of our "aimlessness" and our "intensity" and what is the disastrous outcome of our daily search for a home in this world. First in
society, then in science (chapter seven), and finally in religion (chapter
eight), we begin to appreciate how far we have fallen (chapter nine) from
what was once revealed to humankind and can never truly be lost. For
even while that vision is in eclipse we yet live in its shadow.

The Consumer Index and Human Crisis
Long before I began to notice the kinds of changes I've described in
earlier chapters, this fundamental change in our view of the world—this
world without heaven—and before I began to see how central it was to
the peculiar anxieties of our age, I was beginning to notice something
else. That is, the pressures for consumption, and more consumption, in
our society were giving birth to a radically different way of looking at
human life.

For a meeting of religion professor-types in St. Louis, I wrote a paper, trying to describe what I saw happening—the consumer-driven society, the ecological problems and the emerging crisis in the human self-concept. At the beginning I described the great societal machinery, all geared to serve the interests of ravenously expanding consumption:

> Consumption becomes the burden and purpose of institutions, social relationships, public policy, and a whole blossoming outgrowth of service industries—insurance companies that protect the fragile accumulation of wealth, finance companies that encourage the ever-expanding usurious mortgaging of the future for the sake of the immediate gratification of consumer interests, and an advertising industry that fine-tunes its skill in stimulating an infinitely expandable public appetite for possessions, pleasures, and personal improvement. The virtues of thrift, prudence, simplicity, and self-restraint are passed over by the shrill appeal of the marketplace. Motives that purport not to be based on consumer appetites are met with suspicion and with open contempt. Thus a friend of mine who contended that, while teaching often was not rewarded with large salaries, it had its other nonmaterial compensations, found himself rebuffed by incredulous remarks from co-workers who believed any incentive unrelated to money could be only a "sour grapes" resignation to the prospect of low salaries.[1]

This ravenous approach to life, as we are fast learning, leads to some enormous pressures to make the environment yield all it can, and with disastrous loss to the ecological system. But there is another consequence at least as critical and which in any case shows how far the process has driven us. In the paper I had prepared, I saw it as an integral part of the environmental issue that now human beings are also seen as resources:

> Even the vocabulary by which we refer to social interests reflects this preoccupation with economic exploitation. We speak of the rights of "consumers"—as if consumers are a special segment of the population whose rights must be protected. In fact, however, here is an

element of life that has been abstracted from a more holistic view of human existence and moved from the periphery to the center of social interests. It takes its place alongside the rights to life, liberty, and the pursuit of happiness—which rights were assumed to spring from the idea of natural law. Consumption shifts in status from something that advances the interests of the higher aims of humanity to an inalienable right that must be served. Once we did eat to live; now we live to eat.

Even more auspicious, perhaps, is the multiplication of public agencies that have adopted such titles as "department of human resources." That human beings themselves can be considered "resources"—consumable raw material for public order—is an idea reminiscent of *Brave New World*, and it also augurs a profound shift in the values of a society."[2]

Humanity and Holocaust

Unfortunately, the twentieth century has given us many dramatic examples of a society which feeds upon itself by turning people into resources. Aleksandr Solzhenitsyn has demonstrated throughout his monumental three volumes of *The Gulag Archipelago* how a tyranny was driven by economic "necessity" to consume its own people like so much firewood to assure its own self-perpetuation. Millions, and generations, of Russians, Ukrainians, Jews, Tartars and others were marched to the labor camps and the prisons, kept in internal exile, driven as slave labor, shot to death with slight provocation. "Why did we stand for it?" he asks. In a chapter by that title, he sums up the answer this way:

> Through Stalin's lips our country was bidden henceforth to *renounce complacency*. But under the word complacency Dal [a nineteenth-century lexicographer] gives "kindness of heart, a loving state of mind, charity, a concern for the general good." That was what we were called upon to renounce, and we did so in a hurry—renounced all concern for the general good! Henceforth our own feeding trough was enough for us.[3]

When Helmut Thielicke, the German pastor and theologian, toured the United States in the early sixties, he was questioned about the Nazi holocaust. How could it have happened in Germany, his questioner asked, among people of such obvious accomplishments in learning and culture, and above all in a country of great churches, great theologians and strong historic ties to the Christian faith? He had opposed the rise of Hitler and had experienced how a civilized people could be "dragged over half the earth by a cruel conqueror and then . . . carried along into the same abyss into which he plunges."[4]

His answer to this question included the economic and political conditions of the times, the peculiar circumstances that gave Hitler the opportune moment to seize power, and the deceit and intrigue which all of this involved. However, he said that even when all of this has been discussed it does not fully explain how a people could have fallen victim to Hitler and become implicated in his horrendous crimes.

The most important reason for this "guilt and catastrophe," he said, is theological in nature. It involves "two extremely different views of man." In one a person is seen and evaluated in terms of functional worth: he or she is intelligent, strong, skillful, well trained and educated. Therefore, the scale of values by which a person is judged worthy depends upon what that person contributes to society. This man functions as an engineer, creating greater wealth in society. This woman is beautiful and young, so she bears erotic and aesthetic value for society.

By the same token, those who are ill, handicapped, very old, very young or mentally defective are of less value in terms of social and economic function. From a pragmatic view of society they are consumers but not contributors.

The Nazi regime operated by the logic of this system of values. "Crazy as it may sound," Thielicke said, "these gruesome characters had a code of ethics." As an example, a member of the S.S. refused to take part in a mass execution for "reasons of conscience." He tried to explain this to Himmler, the chief of the S.S. But Himmler, in Thielicke's words, replied in this vein:

It is not your conscience but your weakness that recoils from the horrible. The National Socialist conscience has upon its table of laws certain supreme values such as the purity of the race. From this follows the ethical postulate that all destructive racial elements (Jews) and all inferior life which is merely a hindrance (mental defectives) must be destroyed. Here is where the moral demands which bind your conscience are to be found. Your inhibitions lie either in your cowardice which prevents you from drawing the ethical consequences or in the fact that your conscience has not yet thrown off the remnants of bourgeois, Christian, Mediterranean ideals.[5]

The central point, as you can see, is that even this abysmal "code of ethics" is based upon a system of values that is essentially pragmatic. So Thielicke saw that what had happened in Europe under the Nazis was made possible in the first place by the abandonment of a view of humanity that is nonpragmatic. And since "pragmatic" means nothing more than "serving practical purposes"—in other words, purposes that are very much of this world, which can be known in everyday experience—the meaning of a pragmatic goal is precisely the same as a nontranscendent goal.

The opposite of this functional, pragmatic and nontranscendent view of humanity is "the one we find in the gospel." In the gospel, Thielicke says,

the dignity of man rests not upon his functional ability, but rather upon the fact that God loves him, that he was dearly purchased, that Christ died for him, and that therefore he stands under the protection of God's eternal goodness. . . . Thus Bodelschwingh, the director of an institute for epileptics, could fling himself against the myrmidons of the S.S. and say: "You will take them away [for killing] only over my dead body." He knew that the most wretched of them . . . are loved by God.[6]

This idea of the worth of human life is what Martin Luther referred to as "alien dignity." Our value as human beings does not rest on some intrinsic quality such as beauty or intelligence, nor upon our strength, skill and virtue. Instead our worth, our "dignity," rests upon the fact that we are loved, that we are created in the image of God and that we are destined for reconciliation with him. Human worth, in other words, does not proceed from *strength*, but from grace. It is not earned (pragmatic); it is only received from outside (transcendent). It was the loss of this powerful concept of human dignity that made possible the ruthless devastation of the Holocaust.

Though we have not met with the same kind of crisis as Germany of the thirties and forties, it must be observed that Germany is not alone in abandoning the transcendent for the pragmatic in evaluating human worth.

In a recent editorial appearing in my morning paper, the writer argued that legal and ethical decisions to prolong the life of persons reduced to an irreversible vegetative state and dependent on artificial life-support systems are hampered by what he called "physical fundamentalism." He quoted Karl Barth to the effect that "life is no second God, and therefore the respect due it cannot rival the reverence owed God." Up to this point the writer, Albert Keller, a medical ethicist at the Medical University of South Carolina, made a very interesting point and one fully consistent with belief in transcendent values. "When the value of life is made absolute," he said, "life becomes an idol." And since life is not an end in itself, this means "learning to accept death and other 'conditions of finitude' with grace and dignity."

It struck me that Keller's warnings against "physical fundamentalism," as he called it, were eloquent and on the whole convincing. But when he turned, as he did briefly, to state those positive values that define human life as sacred, the veil of modern nontranscendent values fell over his eyes. Why is life valuable? "It is precious," he said, "because of the ways it can be used and enjoyed."[7] One must conclude that if life is valuable to the extent that it is "used and enjoyed," then those who suffer in some chronic disorder, and who therefore are most in need of help in preserving life, are precisely the ones whose value of life is diminished.

To make matters worse, he quoted a physician named Willard Gaylin to explain why "being human is special." Those attitudes that distinguish us from the beasts, that define our awareness, he said, "must be encouraged and enhanced to *maintain our status* 'in the image of God' " (emphasis mine). The idea of "maintaining our status," of course, is the precise opposite of the biblical teaching that we are created in the image of God. From the Jewish and Christian point of view, the "image of God" is a state from which we have fallen and for which the faithful are destined. And the fact that we are created in that image imposes upon us both a sacred duty and a terrible freedom. But in no sense is the "image of God" something we can "maintain." And though the relationship with God that this implies may be tragically marred and the rebellion from its requirements may end in our own destruction, it cannot be lost, denied, renounced or otherwise disengaged from whom we are.

But for ethicists and physicians to blithely suggest maintaining the image of God through a quality of life that is useful and enjoyable shows how far we have come from being guided by a sense of the transcendent meaning of life.

The ideal "quality of life" is inseparable from the nontranscendent drive to domesticate the world. Once we have assumed that the true rewards of life are here, then the idea of physical or mental handicap, of terminal suffering or even of social incompatibility becomes insufferable. The more the notion arises that life must be complete in this world, the greater is the desire to justify it on the basis of its function in a society whose goals are self-fulfilling. This affects the way we look at life and death at the extreme ranges of life. Millard Everett in his book *Ideals of Life* proposes the following:

> No child [should] be admitted into the society of the living who would be certain to suffer any social handicap—for example, any physical or mental defect that would prevent marriage or would make others tolerate his company only from the sense of mercy.[8]

Everett must assume that calling forth a "sense of mercy" in society is some kind of unwelcome strain on social relations instead of its being—

as it has been considered for most of the era since Christ—the very quality one would want to cultivate in society and which, in fact, makes society possible.

Once the possibility of life based on a transcendent goal has been ruled out, the course of logic follows a predictable and tragic pattern. Malcolm Muggeridge detected this impenetrable, though captive, thinking when he was invited to participate in a BBC program on Dr. Christian Barnard's first heart-transplant operation in Pretoria, South Africa. With great resistance from other panelists and the audience (mostly medical professionals), he tried to probe the issue of whether organ transplant did not entail a cheapening of human life. He asked Dr. Barnard if he was "the first surgeon to chance his arm with a heart-transplant operation, whereas elsewhere there were still qualms and hesitations, because in South Africa the doctrine of apartheid had devalued human flesh, reducing it from something God had deigned to put on, to a mere carcass."

The question, Muggeridge said, was "extremely ill-received," and he found himself unable to evoke even the slightest sympathy from representatives of the medical society, and even the church, who were there, to the idea that there might be adverse results from such unbridled medical efforts to assure the quality of life. To assure a quality of life, that is to be sure, meant achieving a satisfactory experience of life for some people.

Muggeridge's later meditations on Dr. Barnard's autobiography *One Life* are worth quoting at length:

The Barnard experience stayed in my mind, and as I thought about it, I realized that it amounted to a sort of parable illustrating a basic dilemma of our time, as between the sanctity of life as conceived through the Christian centuries, and the quality of life as conceived in a materialist society. Those doctors in the BBC studio rejoicing in the new possibilities in surgery that Dr. Barnard seemed to have opened up, saw human beings as bodies merely, and so capable of constant improvement, until at last perfection was achieved.

No more sick or misshapen bodies, no more disturbed or twisted minds, no more hereditary idiots or mongoloid children. Babies not up to scratch would be destroyed, before or after birth, as would also the old beyond repair. With the developing skills of modern medicine, the human race could be pruned and carefully tended until only the perfect blooms—the beauty queens, the mensa I.Q.'s, the athletes— remained. Then at last, with rigid population control to prevent the good work being ruined by excessive numbers, affliction would be ended, and maybe death itself abolished, and men become, not just like gods, but in their perfect mortality, very God.[9]

Perhaps what is most important in Muggeridge's comments is not so much his implied critique of organ transplantation as his warning against perfectionism, especially its secular expression. Though Christian theology has always struggled with the idea of the call to perfection (for example, in Jesus' words "Be perfect, therefore, as your heavenly Father is perfect," Mt 5:48), it has largely resisted the notion that one finally arrives at a state of completion out of which no more progress is possible.

Thus Augustine and others rejected the perfectionism of the Pelagian error (simply put, "salvation by works"). They saw perfection instead as a "relative perfection" which, as John Calvin expressed it, is "progress in this life." Thus, against the secularized, obsessive drive for perfection—which ends in all manner of personal tragedy and social disaster— stands the Christian focus on a goal outside of life, which involves a longing for more justice, greater harmony and increased love in the present life. From earliest times Christians generally saw that to aim for a nontranscendent perfection invites ruin, while the call to a transcendent goal of perfection lifts standards to ever higher levels. Even John Wesley, whose name is so often associated with Christian perfectionism, saw this idea in terms of daily going "from strength to strength."[10] Still Wesley's implication of this-worldly perfection worried Zinzendorf enough for him to warn Wesley in 1741 that perfection in this life is "the error of errors." "I pursue it through the world," he said, "with fire and sword." Thus the typical Christian expectation of improvement in this life is everywhere encouraged, along with the warning against radical expectations of a temporal state of perfection.

Quality of Life vs. Life

Perfectionism, as opposed to the Christian desire for improvement, is often expressed in the secular and nontranscendent anxiety over a "quality of life." The idea of the "quality of life," so often on the lips of defenders of abortion "rights" as well as advocates of suicide and euthanasia, is not in itself an offensive idea. But in the tortuous ideals of nontranscendent expectations the "quality of life" is necessarily all-important. For if one cannot find the answer to his desires here, then where can he find them? And if a woman, for instance, is burdened with an unwanted pregnancy, then how obviously is the quest for an unfettered and unimpeded life hindered! How can the world possibly tolerate unwanted babies, burdensome older people and sick people? There are already so many, and the chance to discover that life of complete satisfaction is so brief. The measure of suffering, not to mention disappointment, inconvenience, dissatisfaction and frustration, mounts to the sky; yet one only "goes round once."

No problem arises from the quest for a better *quality of life*, even if that term could be defined and agreed upon. The problem arises from the assumption that life is defined by its fulfillment in happiness, harmony, success and comfort or in any number of other desires for the experiences of life.

The most convenient critique of the Christian life has always been that it refuses to focus on the quality of life in this world. Such is a great shame, it is assumed, because what you do not go after, you will not get. The Romans complained that Christians were "enemies of mankind" because of their view that life was desperately intertwined in sin and could only be made right by the action of God himself. The Christians, unlike Roman society, denied the completeness of life apart from God's saving grace. And they also asserted that to become aware of that incompleteness of worldly life—whether through illness, poverty, persecution, humiliation or misfortune—is a part of that grace. "Consider it pure joy, my brothers," said James, "whenever you face trials of many kinds," for in these trials you must suffer with patience. And it is in *that* experience that you become "mature and complete, not lacking anything" (Jas 1:1-4).

Paul spoke regularly of the fact that the greater world did not comprehend the Christian teaching of the cross. Whether by the law (the Jews) or by natural gifts (the Greeks) they attempted to resolve the enigma and the suffering of life directly, whereas Christians embraced trials as opportunities to learn of God and to grow in grace. This teaching is for the Jews, Paul said, a stumbling block, and for the Gentiles it is foolishness. But to those who are called, it is the very essence of Christ, "the power of God and the wisdom of God" (1 Cor 1:13-14).

I once heard G. Gordon Liddy speak to a college audience in Missouri. Throughout the evening this former White House aide, who had been only a short time earlier released from a prison sentence for his part in the famous Watergate episode, urged upon us the idea that only force, strength, ruthless use of violence and an iron will could earn the respect of friends and foes in this "real world which is, in fact, a very tough neighborhood."

I am enough of a "Christian realist" in the tradition of Reinhold Niebuhr to at least appreciate an element of his thinking. After all, the government's role *is* the use of force. And in a fallen world it is needed. But Liddy seemed to mean more than this: force and a strong will for him were not provisional answers in a fallen world; they were the answer.

One of my colleagues on the faculty rose to timidly pose the question: "But, in our country, most people . . . after all . . . do base their ethics on . . . like . . . the teachings of Jesus . . . and" (finally he got it out with a rush) "this-doesn't-sound-much-like-the-teachings-of-Jesus." He sat down.

Liddy glared a moment, took in a breath, and bellowed: "Yeah—and look what happened to Jesus!" He flailed his arms outward, holding them as if on the crossbeam of a gibbet: "They crucified him." To Liddy, the case was closed. The audience reacted, briefly, as if stunned, astonished—and then with thunderous applause. After all, Liddy only said out loud what everyone else had already concluded: "Failure, persecution and pain, instead of success, appreciation and a good retirement—that's no way to end up."

Unlike Liddy and kindred spirits, who wish to control the outside world by force of will, there are those who seek wholeness and harmony within the psyche. By some, our age has been called the therapeutic age, because we have been easily convinced of the need to work at resolving psychological and emotional difficulties. Not only in serious mental or emotional disorders, but in view of much lesser states of general dissatisfaction, our age has been convinced of the need to consult a new kind of priest: the therapist.

Sigmund Freud, of course, stood at the head of this movement. It is significant, I think, that he saw religion (by which he meant principally Judeo-Christian religion) as the major "enemy" of his movement.[11] He saw the reason for this very clearly. For the Christian religion proposed that life without God and without his transcendent goal of life is not, and cannot be, made whole. So his objection is predictable:

> Religion is an attempt to get control over the sensory world, in which we are placed, by means of the wish-world, which we have developed inside us as a result of biological and psychological necessities. But it cannot achieve its end. . . . Its consolations deserve no trust.[12]

One can easily see that Freud, a true product of an age now losing its sense of transcendence, sees as fraudulent any attempt to resolve the various problems of life by appeal to the idea that life is incomplete because it cannot be complete in this world. Though he does not promise a resolution of all problems, he clearly implies that such a resolution in *this* world is the only legitimate human goal.

In these same lectures in which he sees religion as "the chief enemy," it is intriguing that he saw (from a perspective early in the twentieth century) that communism was actually sharing, in a sense, his own view of the world. While he operated to resolve life from within, they moved to convert the economic environment, bringing about a resolution from without. Both of these points of view, however, necessarily imply the need to resolve life's deficiencies. And in this limited sense, they share a common front against religion. So Freud voices his limited support of the communist experiment (which is quite interesting since we know some of the results of that experiment):

> There are also men of action, unshakable in their convictions, impervious to doubt, and insensitive to the sufferings of anyone who stands between them and their goal. It is owing to such men that the tremendous attempt to institute a new order of society of this kind is actually being carried out in Russia now. At a time when great nations are declaring that they expect to find their salvation solely from a steadfast adherence to Christian piety, the upheaval in Russia ... seems to promise a better future.[13]

Finally, however, I want to stress that compared to views of life that seek final resolutions in this life—views held by Freud, by revolutionaries of various stripes, by the G. Gordon Liddys with their romantic views of steel-edged human will and by all of those from ancient times who have asserted that Christianity lacks a concern for this life and the "quality" of this life—the Christian view of the world is the one which seems to have consistently made a better world come to reality. It was precisely those Christians who saw the world as incomplete, painful, sinful and corruptible who had the moral stamina and the patience to do what was needed. Just as perfectionists are paralyzed into inaction because they fear their actions will be faulty, those who anticipate a resolution to significant and age-old problems in life seem to get no further than hand-wringing protests, while those who believe the world to be improvable set to work. And they work with patience and long-suffering because they believe their true goal for both the individual and society is a long way off.

It is very much as Alexis de Tocqueville said nearly two centuries ago:

In ages of faith, the final end of life is placed beyond life. The men of those ages, therefore, naturally and almost involuntarily accustom themselves to fix their gaze for many years on some immovable object toward which they are constantly tending; and they learn by insensible degrees to repress a multitude of petty passing desires in order to be the better able to content that great and lasting desire which possesses them. . . . This explains why religious nations often achieved such lasting results; for whilst they were thinking only of the other world, they had found out the great secret of success in this.[14]

What, then, has lured us so far from this course? The answer is close at hand: science and technology have dramatically come into our lives and the temptation is great to believe that we can, after all, "turn these stones into bread."

CHAPTER 7

SCIENCE AS PRAGMATICS

What is happiness?—The feeling that power
increases—that a resistance is overcome.

Friedrich Nietzsche, *The Anti-Christ*

• • •

THE SUMMER OF 1967 WAS THE SUMMER OF BISHOP JAMES PIKE, WHO MADE HEAD-lines with his notions that Christianity, in its present form, had finally become superannuated. The God-Is-Dead theology of Thomas J. J. Altizer and others was still a live topic a year or more after papers announced that "God Is Dead in Georgia."

A few months earlier, attending a Billy Graham crusade in Greenville, South Carolina, I recall seeing a high-school student with a copy of the book I had seen everywhere that year, John A. T. Robinson's *Honest to God*. The book that argued against the older transcendent pictures of God, and for a theology of secular Christianity, had become a best seller. As the debate over his thesis continued, Robinson would later argue that until now "man has felt the need for God, as a child feels the need for his father. He must be 'there' to explain the universe, to protect him in his loneliness, to fill the gaps in his science, to provide the sanction for his morality."[1]

Honest in *Honest to God* meant no longer pre-scientific, which means more descriptive and less suggestive of "a super-world of divine objects" (Tillich). The fact that God cannot be described but must be alluded to in metaphors, beside the popular notion that science does not use metaphor and describes things directly and seriously (no serious scientist thinks this, of course), left many people at an impasse. They would just drop supernatural language altogether.

That summer I was working, between college and seminary, with a civil defense research group at the University of Georgia. Naturally, a number of scientific and psychological types were there; and the fact that our research dealt with some rather apocalyptic possibilities, combined with the fact that I was on my way to seminary—which marked me as "religious"—frequently turned conversations in that group toward the issue of science and religion.

I remember one discussion in particular. It is the very discussion, naturally, that at one time I would have much preferred to forget.

A bright graduate student in experimental psychology, one of our group, wanted to meet the issue of science and religion head-on. Brenda was twenty-three. She had grown up in the Catholic church and now imagined she had outgrown it.

"Religion is only useful in explaining what we don't yet know." Brenda had a habit of tossing her head back and to the side, swinging her long sixties-style hair off her shoulder to her back. It was a gesture of confidence, as if to say, "Now! It's been said. What will you say to that?"

Her confidence was all the more frustrating when her statement seemed loaded with more assumptions than you could deal with in one sitting. Here was a quick thrust with what I would later call a "God-of-the-gaps" theology. Approaching a statement like that was a bit like trying to pick up a snake; you weren't sure what end to go for first.

Brenda took heart from my delayed answer, a delay that probably betrayed a certain dumbfoundedness on my part. "Human beings," she said, "have a desire to know things and to explain the universe around them. Up till now they have needed religion or something like it; and the more science answers that need, the less we rely upon theology."

We were sitting at a conference table that occupied a central room, with offices and hallways off two sides of the large room. Others from the offices and hallway began to filter in, take a seat and listen in. I was making a lame attempt to "prove" the existence of God. An agency lawyer, hearing the discussion from a distance, rushed in—coffee cup in one hand and a blank sheet of paper in the other. Drawing abstract diagrams, he came to my aid with three of St. Thomas Aquinas's five cosmological arguments for the existence of God.

Brenda, meanwhile, was untroubled. The air of the sophisticate seemed to come naturally to her. She listened politely, but, quietly unimpressed, she tossed her long hair in that brief confident gesture, and pressed on. "The notion of a 'prime mover,' " she said, referring to St. Thomas's argument based on motion, "answered questions as they occurred to medieval theologians. Our questions are different and require a different answer. They were at the mercy of nature, and we are the masters of nature. If someone asks who moves the world, we say, 'Man moves the world.' We want to know how things work and what makes them work; and when we find out, then *we* make them work. We don't know everything now; but what we don't know, we *will* know. The finite realm of that which we do not know grows always smaller, while science makes leaps and bounds."

The conversation gathered momentum. We were joined by a former seminarian, who was now a psychology graduate student, and a law student studying for his bar exam. All of us were working intensely to press forward our particular perspectives. But what indelibly impresses itself upon my memory now are two things. The first is the perfect confidence with which Brenda, and some of the others, discussed religion as irrelevant to any of us now engaged with the real world. Brenda, with the backing not only of scientists and philosophers of the midsixties but also of theologians, stood her ground. The questions of this world and of this age were not religious; they were secular.

The second impression is more difficult to define. But there was already the feeling that it was not religion that suffered from irrelevance, but *this conversation.* We were hiding from something that was terribly apparent, or should have been, to all of us.

In the late afternoon we sat back from the conference table, more reflective than argumentative by now. The agency lawyer's diagrams, on the white sheet of paper, were thrown to the middle of the table. It was time to go back to work. Our work was to investigate, through experiments with masses of volunteers, how people would react to confinement for so many days in a shelter, trying to survive a nuclear holocaust.

On two occasions we housed a thousand or more in makeshift shelters. We watched and counted, and counted again after it was all over. That was the job of the research assistants, to "watch and count." The long enclosures, the leaking chemical toilets, the noisy crowds and the tasteless food were enough to convince me at the time that if ever we were threatened by nuclear attack, a full thirty per cent of the misery would be the dark and the dirt, along with the smell and the noise, of a populated "shelter."

It seems that we brushed up against the more basic question just for a moment. The law student spoke up after listening most of the time. "Brenda," he said, "science gave us atomic weapons."

"Well," said Brenda, "science just gives us knowledge." She hesitated. "It doesn't tell us what . . . to do with it."

"Oh," the law student asked, "then what does?"

It would be years before I heard that kind of question posed as a serious critique of our technological society—a society that had become more and more blind to the fact that even technology has a moral context. What, after all, were we doing there? That's what had not yet dawned on any of us, so intrigued with our abstract questions about religion and science. I had not yet heard of the misgivings some would have regarding science and technology, the ecological crisis, the disappearing ozone layer. Three Mile Island and Chernobyl were years in the future. And while we did make-believe exercises, under the make-believe shadow of the mushroom cloud, we did not ask what Bertrand de Jouvenal asked years later: "Every year," he said, "science and technology allow us to do more and more, until we can now do more than we have ever done before! . . . But what on earth shall we do?"[2]

I was still a child of the mid-twentieth century. It had not occurred to many of us that we could ask any other questions than what is *necessary,* expedient. We were trapped by the walls of technological think-ing, walls that made us forget temporarily that anything other than what is "useful" had any importance. If knowledge exists, it is *for us,* it is for our use and to our glory. "Man moves the world!" seemed pre-posterous even then. But as rhetoric it worked; and I didn't know why.

Pragmatism and Disorientation

About an hour after takeoff, the story goes, a pilot announced to his passengers that his news for them was both good and bad. "First the good news," he said. "We're making good time. But the bad news is . . . we're lost."

The technological and scientific story of the twentieth century might remind you of that wandering airline with throttles set at full speed. The "how to" side of human knowledge is of value only to the extent that it accomplishes a worthy purpose—and the value of *purpose* belongs to that order of thinking that examines the context of an action rather than the action itself. It deals with the ends rather than the means.

Allen Tate has said that secularism is when the means replaces the ends.[3] The success of science has been so spectacular that this has been precisely the effect: the ends have been replaced by the extraordinary means.

We would fail to see our age clearly, in fact, if we didn't acknowledge that the huge advances we have witnessed in science and technology are powerfully seductive. The fact that these advances have brought abun-dant good—they have increased prosperity, eased pain, conquered the skies, multiplied information and generally increased the material pros-pects of life—does not alter the case. Indeed, it strengthens it. As Augustine pointed out, temptation does not come from attraction to evil but from our attraction to something that is so good that we are tempted to love it too much. Science has presented us with that kind of good. It has operated so powerfully upon our lives, and for the most part in good ways, that we are tempted to place it upon a throne and worship it.

Back when technology proceeded along more modest lines it was assumed that action responded to the larger context of reality; now, when actions can be so stupendous in power and effect, one is tempted to think that reality responds to the action. From artificial lights to air conditioning and instant communication, the natural environment is made to seem entirely manageable—until an earthquake, a hurricane or some other calamity wakes us from our technological dream.

Higher Education Succumbs to Pragmatism and Power

Of course, if science and technology have deflected our vision away from the ends and the purpose of human action, it has traditionally been the concern of higher education to examine and conserve that very aspect of human thought. From the time of Socrates' academy, it has been considered the work of education primarily to enable learners to exercise wisdom. Skill in the crafts and the management of institutions are of great importance to society, but since these abilities are specialized they are not capable of dealing with the general aims of society and the individual. They can know "how," but they are not suited to tell "what" and "why." Once the goal has been determined, the craftspeople and the managers make their contribution; but those with an understanding of general principles—which they have gained through the study of the humanities—help to discover the moral context, the purpose and the goal.

Such aptitude requires the study of contexts of human life: history, literature, philosophy, ethics, religion. Even today, in colleges and universities, we maintain a core curriculum of liberal studies, which help to answer the broader questions of human existence and not the narrower questions of technique and method. Against greater and greater pressures to offer "practical" courses of study, college faculties and administrators have never entirely let go of the traditional core curriculum, even though many, if we listen to their rhetoric, are hard pressed to know why.

In a secular society the centrifugal force continually presses away from the center out to the periphery, from the essential question of purpose to the peripheral question of the means and the technique. It is a shift from questions of life itself at the center to questions of "making a living" at the periphery. One can see the effect of these pressures on college campuses everywhere. Using Cornell University as an early example, Allan Bloom described the problem as it appeared in university studies:

> The six-year Ph.D. program, richly supported by the Ford Foundation, was directed specifically to high school students who had already made "a firm career choice" and was intended to rush them through to the start of those careers. A sop was given to desolate humanists in the form of money to fund seminars that these young careerists could take on their way through the College of Arts and Sciences. . . . The Cornell plan for dealing with the problem of liberal education was to suppress the students' longing for liberal education by encouraging their professionalism and their avarice, providing money and all the prestige the community had available to make careerism the center piece of the university.[4]

Bloom insists that in focusing on careerism and professionalism and abdicating its role in the humanities, the arts and the sciences, the university has abandoned its major contribution to society. Because there, in an undergraduate education in particular, is where the great variety of actions, careers, aspirations, appetites and associations can be thought of in terms of the life of the spirit—the life of value and moral context.

Pragmatism and Passivity

By the end of the nineteenth century it was evident that a feeling for the permanence of values was disappearing. Of course, none of the most thoughtful members of a Christian society ever considered civilizational forms themselves (that is, the means by which our values are expressed) to be unchanging. But they did consider that whatever were the values that culture communicated had to do with eternal matters and not with the endless flux of history.

This changing sentiment is often described in terms of a philosophical shift. The romanticism and pragmatism that dominated the turn of the century, especially in Great Britain, Europe and America, were also deeply rooted in the shift toward a thoroughly anthropocentric philosophy led by Descartes in the seventeenth century. Whatever the roots of this change, its character was one of describing values as a product of the human will. At one time they were considered to be discovered or revealed. Now they were, more and more, thought to be produced. Things are not loved because they are precious, but they are precious because we love them.

There is an element of this philosophical story, however, that I think is often overlooked. It is the fact that this shift toward anthropocentric values was accompanied by an unparalleled increase in technological possibilities. The world did indeed begin to look as if it might surrender to the onslaught of the applied sciences. It was an opportune moment for the emergence of a philosophy that exalts human will during the lifetime of Friedrich Nietzsche (1844-1900) and of a sociology of religion that questions the absolute nature of values during the time of Max Weber (1864-1920).

It is no accident, moreover, that the dominant philosophy of the first part of the twentieth century in America—where technological advances were making their greatest impact—was pragmatism. In this philosophy the adequacy of an idea is determined by its consequences. This means, of course, two things. First, the consequences must be knowable, and they must therefore be a part of, and confined to, the sensible world. Second, the notion of consequences—even if the fact is not mentioned—has a *subject:* that is, "consequences" means that some effect is brought about to someone or something, and presumably it makes a difference who that subject is. If I say a certain theory of economics justifies high tariffs against foreign imports, then the practical adequacy of that theory may depend upon whether you are an American manufacturer or a Japanese. It must be assumed, at some level, that the "subject" of pragmatism is the individual, the family, the tribe, the nation, all human beings or all of nature. The results of pragmatic theory cannot be divorced from that decision because values will be determined differently as long as there are different points of reference in regard to the consequences of an action.

Pragmatism, therefore, is precisely a refined articulation of nontranscendence. Both the idea of knowable results and consequences that are viewed in terms of the interests of some subject—even though the subject may not be specified but only implied and even though the subject is as broad as the universe itself—confines values to the circle of this world. And, as we have seen, once we insist upon this point the circle tends to become smaller and smaller, not larger.

The reason pragmatism tends to be reduced to mere egotism is not difficult to see. First, the ends are replaced by means. However broadly we draw the scope of the practical results of an action, we still are speaking of the action itself when we speak of the success or the adequacy of a particular practice: the "end" for which an action served has been *assumed*, but it has not been questioned or investigated. The discussion of an "end" or "goal" is replaced by the process itself. Note, for instance, John Dewey's concept of the "goals":

> Not health as an end fixed once for all, but the needed improvement in health—a continual process—is the end and good. . . . Not perfection as a final goal, but the ever-enduring process of perfecting, maturing, refining is the aim of living. . . . Growth itself is the only moral "end."[5]

Dewey does not mention, here, that the very idea of "growth," "maturing," "refining" and especially "perfecting" implies a before and an after, a lesser and a greater; it implies gradations and therefore implies a standard or goal. So to say that "growth itself is the only moral aim" is only to say that the aim remains unannounced. Therefore the second implication is that, apart from a stated aim, the only other possible standard is the power or impact of the action itself. It means, in the language of political action, that might makes right. For the judgment of a right action or a proper action can only be decided on the level of force, power and effect.

Only at this stage do we see the connection with gross egotism. Because here it becomes apparent that although the subject of an action may be obscured, there is in fact a subject. And if by the "success" or the pragmatic value of an action we mean that it serves the benefits that it intends, then we have only to ask the question, Whose interest? And if the answer is "Why, the commonweal," or "the people," or "the whole of nature," we must still ask within a pragmatic vision of the world, who precisely has decided what is best for the world. And we are necessarily given the answer, "Whoever has the values that prevail!" In short, the whole issue is ultimately decided on the basis of a power struggle and the contest of wills.

Discomforting things begin to happen for the pragmatist, however, once questions like "whose practical interests?" are raised. In a puppet show the puppeteer remains hidden if the show is to be at all convincing. Just so, pragmatists speak often in the passive voice. A pragmatist such as John Herman Randall defends his view against a dualistic interpretation of reality (one that espouses "heaven," "the supernatural," "God," "revelation") by saying that "in contrast to this confusion of metaphysics and practice [moral law and ethical action], empirical naturalism insists that metaphysics is the account of what experience finds in nature [whose experience is not specified], and that practical philosophy is the account of what experience finds [the same lapse] to be good or sought for, to be bad and avoided [sought for and avoided by whom?]."[6]

Like the puppeteer, the subject of any action remains carefully concealed. And, as for the purpose of the action—the goal, the *telos*—the monkey with the cup only appears when the show is over. Until that time, one could almost believe that the show *was* the purpose. To keep on in that analogy, however, the more spectacular the production the less we are likely to ask the Bertrand de Jouvenal question: "Every year we can do more and more . . . but what on earth shall we do?" And never in the history of the world have we witnessed a more impressive production: modern science has truly presented itself in spectacular fashion. Never has it seemed more irrelevant to ask, "What is this all about?" "What is our aim?" Surely, we all thought, such progress is its own justification.[7] And we hardly ever asked—at least, before Hiroshima, Chernobyl and other nuclear disasters—where we were going.

When science (knowledge, in other words) is reduced to that which can only be judged by its effect, then it becomes only an instrument of the will. John Randall readily admitted this when he said that "knowledge . . . functions itself as an instrument in the manipulation of nature, it is a tool whereby natural events are transformed into the means of attaining goods and avoiding evils."[8] His idea of knowledge as an "instrument" of power over nature has the same ring as Descartes' statement that science was to make men "masters and possessors of nature." The shift that has taken place here is not even subtle, but we have grown so accustomed to the hubris connected with science and technology that we tend not even to notice. The shift consists in the fact that whereas knowledge or science was first considered to be the province of intellect, it is now discussed as a province of the will. The discussion of science has shifted from the discovery of truth to the invention of truth—to the "manipulation" of nature.

The further, and more important, implication is that in science-as-an-intellectual-discovery, the center and subject of the endeavor is nature, the "otherness" of a reality outside of the individual. In science-as-pragmatic-instrument, the center and subject is the human will, and nature becomes seen as merely the field into which that will is extended.

Jürgen Moltman, among others, has noted how modern scientific and technological societies have become increasingly greedy for power. The more that is produced, the more the frontiers of pain and disease are pushed back, the more nature is harnessed to increase wealth, the more we discover the "need" for greater power. Earlier civilizations, including Western civilization, Moltman points out, were "highly complicated systems of equilibrium—equilibrium in the relationships between human beings and nature, equilibrium in the relationship between human being and human being, and equilibrium in the relationship between human beings and 'the gods.' " It was, in a word, relationships that commanded the greatest reverence and value in society. However, Moltman continues:

> It is only modern civilizations which, for the first time, have set their sights on development, expansion and conquests. The acquisition of power, the increase of power, and the securing of power: these together with the pursuit of happiness, may be termed the values that actually prevail in modern civilization.[9]

We cannot stop, however, with the description that modern societies hunger for power as if there were something uniquely aberrant in that—as if this attitude toward science, and the conquests of technology, descended upon us from philosophical miscalculations or from the wayward habits of a society that is self-evidently unique only because it is modern. Instead we see the presence—a progressively stronger presence—of a range of power that tempts us to believe that the world can be made a *home* for us. The age-long dream of harmony in a world without the pains and threats of mortal existence, in which final resolutions take place, is held out to us as if it were a fulfillment of the prophecy that "every tear" shall be wiped away—'There will be no more death or mourning or crying or pain, for the old order of things has passed away" (Rev 21:4).

This *too* is a vision of harmony, and our society like any other dreams of that harmony. Only ours—unlike any before—is more powerfully tempted to think that it should not have to allow for those pains, accidents, misfortunes and injustices that prevent this world from satisfying the deepest longing of the human heart. Heaven has faded in both our dreams and our wakefulness because we hope yet to escape the pain of mortality. At the same time science seems to enhance those prospects.

Science and the Deadliness of Power

Yet there is a snare in this worldly dream. The power by which we hope to make up for the defects of existence operates upon relationships in the same way as any other coercive power. As a practical power it does not build relationship, but abridges it by co-opting the power of nature: it does not commune with nature; it manipulates nature. Science—as an applied power—is an extension of the will.

As we have seen before, the character of coercive power is always, in its initial form, destructive. It seeks to overcome the otherness of things and persons. It overcomes the resistance of other wills, other forms, other actions. It tends to reduce all things to the simplicity of the single will. It is the extension of ego—the "I"—as it overcomes diversity with the compactness of a nontranscendent *one*.

That is not to say that coercive power is not necessary, or even, in a fallen world, desirable. In the Old Testament, the law, which operates through the force of obligation and even coercion, enforces a certain order upon the world and thereby makes a space for relationship (love) to thrive. Otherwise the chaos of a lawless society would reduce every association to a power struggle. Nevertheless, it must be kept in mind that the operation of the law is destructive not creative ("the law brings wrath," Paul said in Romans 4:15). In the same way, technology enforces an order upon nature, and its conquests create the possibilities of a more vigorous, inventive life. But to rely upon applied science itself as a solution to the tensions of life is to resolve a problem that is rooted in relationship by abridging and, in effect, ending relationships. That is to say, applied science as a *means* enhances life only to the degree that it is clearly subordinate to just and proper *ends*. Yet it is precisely with regard to ends that science and technology remain unavoidably blind. It is this inevitable dilemma in a technologically sophisticated society that Albert Einstein referred to when he said that our age is one of "perfect means and confused ends."

Aldous Huxley's *Brave New World* envisions a society that takes equilibrium and painlessness provided by science as the supreme value.

Childbirth is eliminated as babies are "decanted" in laboratories. A sterile world is preserved from the terrible tensions of life through drugs and saved from the turmoil of relationships (no marriage, no lasting relationships, everyone belongs to everyone else). The frustrations of delayed satisfaction are eliminated as far as possible. The "decanted infant" cries, and a nurse immediately appears with a bottle of "external secretion." "Feelings lurk in that interval of time between desire and its consummation," the narrator explains: "shorten that interval, break down all those unnecessary barriers." Mustapha Mond, the resident controller for Western Europe—and a theoretician of this new world—lectures a group of schoolboys:

"Consider your own lives," said Mustapha Mond. "Has any of you ever encountered an insurmountable obstacle?"

The question was answered by a negative silence. "Has any of you been compelled to live through a long time-interval between the consciousness of a desire and its fulfillment?"

"Well," began one of the boys, and hesitated.

"Speak up," said the D.H.C. [Director of Hatcheries and Conditioning]. "Don't keep his lordship waiting."

"I once had to wait nearly four weeks before a girl I wanted would let me have her."

"And you felt strong emotion in consequence?"

"Horrible!"

"Horrible; precisely," said the Controller. "Our ancestors were so stupid and short-sighted that when the first reformers came along and offered to deliver them from those horrible emotions, they wouldn't have anything to do with them."[10]

But what they were being delivered from, as Huxley points out in this tale, is not only the tensions within life but also the whole idea of a purpose *for* life. Mustapha Mond reviews a paper written by a biologist and finds it brilliant but heretical, because it introduces the idea of "purpose." He writes "Not to Be Published" across the paper and has the author sent to a remote biological laboratory:

A pity, he thought, as he signed his name. It was a masterly piece of work. But once you began admitting explanations in terms of purpose—well, you didn't know what the result might be. It was the sort of idea that might [make the higher castes] lose their faith in happiness as the Sovereign Good and take to believing, instead, that the goal was somewhere beyond, somewhere outside the human sphere; that the purpose of life was not the maintenance of well-being, but some intensification and refining of consciousness, some enlargement of knowledge.[11]

The thought that this idea of purpose might, after all, be true, crosses his mind. He senses, in fact, that he might be eliminating something significant in life. " 'What fun it would be,' he thought, 'if one didn't have to think about happiness.' "

Nathaniel Hawthorne also saw that the attempt to control life—which is the peculiarly seductive element in technological science—was also a threat to life. In "The Birthmark" he tells of a brilliant young scientist who married a beautiful woman. She was so beautiful and he was so devoted to her beauty that he was all the more offended by one flaw: a birthmark—very small, and in the shape of a man's hand—on her cheek. He determined to invent a concoction that would rid her of this despised flaw. But when he gave her the brew, as it turned out, it both erased the flaw and took her life.

The attempt to perfect life is deadly because it attempts to achieve self-sufficiency. It presents the opportunity to resist relationship, because self-sufficiency implies that relationship is not needed. The modern world of technological powers only needs the insight that the desire for perfect equilibrium without God is the desire to resist life itself. The seductiveness of modern science gains its power, in part, from the desire to sink back into the equilibrium of a lifeless state. It is the death wish of modern nontranscendent society.

CHAPTER 8

RELIGION
AS OBSESSION

We must not exploit our Faith by advertising
it as a technique for achieving earthly
satisfactions. The Faith is not a recipe and
not a program. It is a Way. Recipes and
programs are made to help you carry out
earthly jobs successfully. But a Way is
something you walk in.

Harry Blamires, *The Secular Heresy*

• • •

SOME TIME AGO A COLLEAGUE SENT ME AN ARTICLE CLAIMING THAT THERE ARE
signs of rapid new growth in church attendance in America. This trend,
unlike some earlier upswings in religion, shows a strong relationship to
anxieties caused by the downward spiral of social disintegration, along
with feelings of personal isolation and powerlessness. In other words,
the break-up of the family, the social fallout of rapidly spreading drug
addiction, racial strife and escalating violence have seemed to actually
stimulate the return to religion.

Such a reaction is not surprising; but for Christians there is also
something disconcerting in all this. Here in American society we find
two strong, but totally incongruous, trends. For there is no doubt that

this "return to religion" is heartfelt and genuine. Yet the melancholy fact is that it has so far failed to produce anything resembling a counter-movement in moral values; and not only that, it is actually fueled by the general social decay and personal estrangement. Moreover, church bodies at the national level often appear willing to accommodate trends in moral disintegration by providing theological justification.

Evidence accumulates, therefore, that a society grounded in Christian institutions—as they are now constituted—is incapable of meeting the kinds of crises we find on every side today. The fragmented remains of "Christendom," of a Christian society, are now too dissolute, too irreparably compromised, too unsure of the future to inspire hope or to allay fears. The glory has departed, though the institutions themselves remain and even prosper. Huge numbers make their pilgrimages to the holy places, but they do not find the power there that once was promised.

These seemingly contrary trends are not altogether new. Three decades ago the president of Union Theological Seminary, Henry Van Dusen, began to raise questions about the huge 1950s influx into the church. One feature of this trend toward religion, he said, has a disquieting effect:

> The "revival in religion" has, thus far, been paralleled by no corresponding resurgence or recovery of morality. Just here is the most disturbing, confounding contradiction of our present moral and spiritual situation. If one could plot the complex and illusive data on a graph, the curve of religious vitality and the curve of moral health would be seen to be moving in opposite directions—that of *religion*, upward; that of *morality*, downward. In a sentence, in contemporary America, *religion* is gaining ground; *morality* is steadily losing ground.[1]

This observation by Van Dusen was so striking that the entire next issue of the *Union Seminary Quarterly* carried responses from several of the country's most distinguished thinkers. The trend in formal religious affiliation, of course, fluctuates. But generally, throughout this century we are faced with a profound and troubling paradox. For some reason, as Will Herberg stated the matter concerning the American people, we can be seen at *one and the same time* as the most secular of societies and the most religious of societies.[2] Why the seeming contradiction?

The Rise (Return?) of Nontranscendent Religion

Those who expected to see science displace religion—like Brenda with the civil defense research group—must have suffered rude shocks from time to time. What they have seen instead are regular eruptions in society of religious movements, each one growing with intensity and fanaticism, even as the progress of science increased. Today it is impossible to think about international politics without being aware of intense religious loyalties that are shaping the political landscape.

These are not merely the irrational reactions of people who long for a more primitive world: otherwise the outbreaks of religious fervor would grow steadily weaker. Instead, there is another explanation. The unparalleled interest in religion which we find in the modern world is not abating but increasing, and furthermore, it *parallels* and *imitates* the growing reliance upon technological power. The remarkable concurrence of technology and religion can only be understood as two manifestations of a common social phenomenon. This phenomenon hinges on the fact that, in a limited but extremely important sense, faith in science and faith in religion as a power share precisely the same world vision.

The Reaction

By the late 1960s, when Brenda and Bishop Robinson were giving up on the supernatural, that frankly nonreligious view of the world had about run its course. It was always skating on thin ice, and there were always those who questioned the facile optimism of scientific triumph. But a reaction of an altogether unsuspected kind was in the wind. The late sixties and early seventies was a time of the "escape from reason," a return to mystery: it was the "dawning of the Age of Aquarius."

In April 1966, *Time* magazine appeared with a black cover and the words *Is God Dead?* Three years later, in August 1969, *Time's* cover bore the words *Is God Coming to Life Again?* And in October of 1975 the cover featured an Indian guru named Maharishi Mahesh Yogi. What had appeared to be a movement in society that left religion behind was transposed, in a moment, into a frenzied fascination with religions, and not necessarily with the Christian religion, though that was included, but with all kinds of religions as well as quasi-religious practices such as transcendental meditation.

As it turned out, this was not a brief impulse in society. Over a period of decades the interest has continued. The head of a philosophy department at a nearby state university has recently begun introducing courses in religious studies into the curriculum. He told me that whereas these would probably have met with much indifference when he was in college, today's students fill the classes to capacity. "I can always count on a religion elective being filled," he told me. State colleges and universities throughout the country are having similar responses. New departments in religious studies have sprung up, not just in church-related colleges where they are expected, but in such secular institutions as Missouri University, University of Georgia, Florida State University, Southwest Missouri State and Iowa University. Religion courses are offered out of the philosophy or history department at many other state institutions.

At the older, traditional schools, with a long history of religious studies, the programs are taking on new vitality. At Harvard, Harvey Cox offered a lecture series on "the moral teachings of Jesus," and the enrollment came to almost a thousand.

I can testify from personal experience, teaching at both a state university and a private denominational college, that although many of the humanities have lost support in recent years, and while the business and engineering classes increase, I have never found any lack of interest in religion. The real question is whether that interest is not, on the part of some, actually somewhat frenzied and obsessive.

The diffuse and irregular nature of this religious ferment is seen in many areas. Note, for instance, some common observations about trends in various media:

(1) The list of books from "secular" publishers has shown increasing interest in the religious market. But it is often directed toward a market with decidedly unorthodox tastes.

A few days ago I stopped by my local bookstore, within walking distance of Old Dorchester. I found there a huge department of books on "Religion and the Occult." Shelf upon shelf was devoted to life after death, reincarnation, psychic powers, magic and so on. I wrote down a few of the titles: *The Unknown Reality* by Jane Roberts (through whom "Seth" reveals the "intimate secrets of our existence"), *Satan Wants You, Meditations for the New Age, How to Meditate* (a guide to self-discovery), *Develop Your Psychic Abilities, A Complete Guide to the Tarot, ESP for Everyone, Death and Consciousness: The Case for Life After Death, Your Past Lives: A Reincarnation Handbook.*

(2) The newspaper industry is, of course, highly sensitive to popular tastes, especially at the local level. The editor of a large daily newspaper said recently that he never received so much protest from readers over the elimination of any feature as when he tried to cut an astrology column! The former First Lady, Nancy Reagan, admitted that she consulted regularly with an astrologer; and it was alleged that she used astrological nostrums to influence her husband's schedule.

(3) In music and entertainment the fascination with religion takes many forms, including an interest in magic, witchcraft, spiritualism and a range of occult arts. Every semester I meet students who have been influenced by these interests. The music of youth, rock music, makes steady reference to nothing so regularly as religion—not orthodox Christian religion, of course, but religion nonetheless. Everything from blasphemy to hero worship is found in the prominent pieces of the rock age. Robert Pattison's excellent study of rock music calls attention to the religious interests of the genre:

> Some rock, like the songs of Soft Cell, is overtly Christian; other rock, like the Feederz's "Jesus Entering from the Rear," is blasphe-

mous; and still other rock, like the music of the Police, is arguably Christian and atheistical all at once. There is Vedic rock, Zen rock, Rastafarian rock, born-again rock, never-born rock, and thanks to Kinky Friedman and the Texas Jewboys, even Jewish rock, each distinguished by its vulgar treatment of its religious material. Rock's pantheism happily accommodates the varieties of religious experience, careless of whatever contradictions arise, and on the *Billboard* album charts a record by U2 that features lead singer Bono's adaptation of the Gloria from the mass appears next to Motley Crue's *Shout at the Devil*.[3]

It seems clear that the cultures of drug craving, rock music and occult practices all have one thing in common—an intense religious preoccupation, one that is mirrored, as we have seen, in every area of the media. This interest in religion seems not less real for being obsessive, diverse and frequently destructive. The situation we find in the late twentieth century reminds me of G. K. Chesterton's remark somewhere that when people stop believing in God they do not believe in nothing—they'll believe anything.

The Contradictions of a "Religious" Culture

This intense religious interest presents us with confusing and contradictory signals concerning the nature of our times. We have become used to saying that our culture is secular. But the very presence of a secular—or, I might say, the absence of a transcendent—feeling for life seems to bring forth, not irreligion, but a supercharged fascination with religion.

Ironically, the most secular of cultures, our own, is linked to a fascination for religion that is perhaps unparalleled in human experience. Logarithms and lectionaries, spacecraft and spook-lore, Satan and satellites—all spinning around in the same modern minds and filling the same electronically charged airways.

This situation should make us wonder if we have posed the alternatives correctly. The idea of secularism as a "way of living and thinking"—not simply as an expression for living "in the world"—includes the Enlightenment idea of autonomy, of living on one's own.

Religion, however, will not necessarily be hostile to that ideal of self-rule. In fact, the more intimately we become acquainted with the effort to find, within ourselves, the resources to live "on our own," the more we may find the need to call upon any "power" that offers to come to our aid. Religion may present itself as an ally to our efforts at independence. It can promise to continue the struggle to stand apart, to live as a consumer of the world's riches, as hidden from God and as free from the responsibilities for a brother. Like secularism, it can be only a better way to seek my own.

The question becomes, Is the truth of the tension in human life described by the alternatives "secular" and "religious"? Or is there another way that offers a criticism of *both* the secular and the religious efforts that have promised to support a stubborn and rebellious *ego*?

Two Kinds of Religion

An answer might be found in one of the oldest, most sustained and most successful efforts to criticize the prevailing religious culture of a people. Of the great efforts to penetrate to the core of human experience, such as the Greek philosophical movement, only one has been a sustained polemic against the religious habits and opinions of its generation. That is the Hebrew prophetic movement.

In large part, the Bible is a product of that movement. The argument that we find underlying that movement, from Moses to Malachi, is that a religion that merely serves the interest of a person, a tribe or a nation falls short of the full meaning of the worship of God.

King Saul, the first king of a united Israel, is a supreme example. In 1 Samuel we find him in full possession of all the requisite virtues of the ideal monarch—kingly stature, military prowess and ordination by God through the prophet/priest/judge Samuel. The greater part of Saul's story, in the prophetic history of Israel, however, is the story of his fall. Three distinct accounts tell of his rejection as king.

In the first one we find him hard-pressed by an aggressive Philistine army near Gilgal. Patiently, at least for a time, he waits for Samuel to come and offer the sacrifice so the army can go forth into battle. Clearly Saul is concerned that the religious rite be observed, and just as clearly he thinks this is a prerequisite to killing Philistines. Then, though he is not himself a priest, and has no right to do so, he begins to offer the sacrifice. And Samuel comes upon the scene:

> "What have you done?" asked Samuel. Saul replied, "When I saw that the men were scattering, and that you did not come at the set time, and that the Philistines were mustering at Micmash, I thought, 'Now the Philistines will come down against me at Gilgal, and I have not sought the LORD's favor.' So I felt compelled to offer the burnt offering." (1 Sam 13:11-12)

Notice, first of all, that Saul argues for the *expediency* of his situation. And his argument is a strong one; as a matter of fact, from the point of view of the religious Israelite, it is unassailable. And notice, second, that it is basically a religious argument. In Saul, religion and expediency cross paths—they are, in effect, one and the same. That is, in fact, for the prophets, the common thread running through pagan religious life, and it is the very core of their criticism: for the worship of the God of Israel proceeds not from the needs of the people (expediency) but from the worthiness of God. He is to be obeyed, not because it is good for the people, but because he is God.

Two other episodes in the life of Saul follow a similar pattern. Saul acts in disobedience to God, but his actions are clearly religious in nature. His act of obedience would have been inexpedient, but the pragmatic aim of his disobedient actions is justified on religious and cultic grounds. He imposed a fast upon the people, binding them to a religious oath but causing them to disobey the prohibition against "eating meat with blood still in it." He refused to slaughter much of the cattle and sheep of the Amalekites, as well as King Agag, as he was commanded to do, because he was saving the best for a special sacrifice. In each case Saul is expedient, pragmatic and clearly religious; but, in each case, he is disobedient.

Samuel's response to Saul's repeated disobedience reveals the heart of the prophetic revolt against religion as an expedient:

> Does the LORD delight in burnt offerings and sacrifices as much as in obeying the voice of the LORD? To obey is better than sacrifice, and to heed is better than the fat of rams. For rebellion is like the sin of divination, and arrogance like the evil of idolatry. Because you have rejected the word of the LORD, he has rejected you as king. (1 Sam 15:22-23)

As the prophets saw, the God of Israel imposed demands of a different order from those perceived by other nations. Their religion constituted a different approach to life. Religion as a general practice, or a way of getting on in the world, is what they saw among their neighbors, even among their Israelite neighbors. The religion of the pagans was, as they saw it, a quid pro quo religion. Religion was not, in the first place, a theology or a faith so much as it was a practice, an act, a cult. And the cult had a purpose—it was to grow more crops, produce greater flocks, ward off evil, impregnate wives, increase wealth, survive war and disease, and bring down calamity upon the enemy.

For the prophet, the quid pro quo was incidental, not central. The meaning of religion was captured in the obedience to God. Disease, suffering, death, the triumph of one's enemy, childlessness, poverty, famine and a host of evils might intervene, but obedience was central. In fact the story of Israel is, in effect, the story of a people who suffer one disaster after another—not one success after another—as they are pressed into the service of God. And the evils are endurable because they serve a greater purpose, perhaps a purpose that is known only to God and one that ultimately redounds to the glory of God.

For Israel's pagan neighbors, moreover, religion was in the cult itself. It was often seen as an act which they initiated in order to appeal to the god, for purposes that are clear, concrete and very much of this world. For the Hebrew prophets religion is conceived, first of all, as God's initiative, appealing to humans to cooperate in serving a purpose that they often cannot see or understand. Pagan religion quite often appealed to motives of human expediency. The religion of the prophets was inexpedient in the extreme.

This ideal of the inexpedient religion—a religion founded on obedience alone—was happily illustrated in a conversation between Reinhold Niebuhr, the Protestant theologian, and the great Jewish thinker Abraham Heschel. Niebuhr asked Heschel, "Do you keep all of the Jewish dietary laws?"

Heschel answered, "I try to keep *all* of them."

"Why?" Niebuhr asked.

"I'll give you what you might consider a very strange answer, my friend," said Heschel. "I keep all the dietary laws because I don't know the reason for them."

The essence of prophetic religion was faithfulness to a God whose purposes transcended human purposes and whose commands were based upon a reality that was incalculably greater that human comprehension. Though, of course, one risks gross oversimplification in doing so, a chart such as the following might illustrate the difference between the two kinds of religion. The tendency of pagan/popular religion is to see people enlisting the gods (or God) in their own practical purposes:

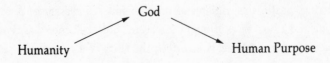

The prophetic religion understands God as enlisting humankind in his unknown and unforeseen purposes:

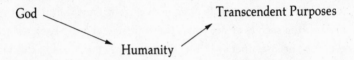

This great insight of the prophets, which they pursued with every ounce of energy over a period of centuries and which gave birth both to

Judaism and to Christianity, drove a wedge forever between two kinds of religion. It would not be wrong to say that one is pagan and the other is first Jewish, then Christian. But that way of putting the matter obscures the fact that all religion, and every practice of religion, and in fact all of human life, is in danger of being marshaled into the service of the human ego.

That is what the prophets understood more profoundly than anyone else. The danger of the Baal worship, as an influence upon Israel, consisted in the fact that their own God (who was sometimes identified with Baal in the popular mind) might be seen no longer as the one who made the fertile world, but rather as the one who makes the world fertile. Rather than understanding God as the meaning in all things, he becomes the means by which we gain some things. Rather than a God to be worshiped, he becomes a god to be used.

With this diminished concept of God, all things become swallowed up in the general utilitarian spirit. And the utilitarian spirit is nothing more than, and nothing other than, selfishness. The object of utilitarianism is always "me." It may be a collective "me," or an individual "me," but it is that which serves self. The prophets recognized that life itself has been sacrificed when there is no longer that which is worthy in and of itself. To say that we worship God is to say that God's worth does not derive from his value to us as a "means" to make life better or happier. By extension, those whom God loves and that which God has created do not need to be justified by their function, or their use, but they have value in and of themselves.

Passion and Obsession

I want to point out, however, that although the prophetic religion of Israel and the faith of the early church did not rely on the common sense of utilitarian motives, it was enormously powerful in motivating radical changes. In fact, precisely because it didn't rely on these motives (which are naturally tempered by self-interest and caution) it demonstrated the highest capacity for changing society.

What was required for this powerful transformation was passion. As Hegel observed, "Nothing great in the World was ever accomplished without passion." And it is that *passion* which Christians exhibited in greatest measure—not Aristotelian balance or Stoic impassibility, but a passion for Christ and a love of people, brought on by the presence and power of the Holy Spirit. This passion is exuded by biblical writers in the most forceful and uncompromising language. John wrote, for instance:

> In this the children of God are manifest, and the children of the devil: whosoever doeth not righteousness is not of God, neither he that loveth not his brother. (1 Jn 3:10 KJV)

The "doing of righteousness," therefore, is summed up in the loving of others, and this is the measure of the Christian life: "We know that we have passed from death unto life, because we love the brethren" (v. 14).

But what John says about the *measure* by which we love each other only fails to shock us now because we have gotten used to biblical language. The thing that we should see here is how utterly *immoderate*—as well as unpragmatic—is his criterion for knowing if the love of God is evidenced in a Christian: "Hereby perceive we the love of God, because he laid down his life for us: and we ought to lay down our lives for the brethren" (v. 16).

The language of the New Testament has grown tame by usage and by the very temperate environments in which we hear these words; after all, many of us hear these words first from *proper* Sunday-school teachers and from ministers who are the quintessence of civil decorum. And yet, when people first heard them, they absolutely must have had the sound and feeling of a call to arms:

> Dear friends, do not be surprised at the painful trial you are suffering, . . . But rejoice that you participate in the sufferings of Christ. . . . However, if you suffer as a Christian, do not be ashamed, but praise God that you bear that name. For it is time for judgment to begin with the family of God. . . . So then, those who suffer according to God's will should commit themselves to their faithful Creator and

continue to do good. (1 Pet 4:12-13, 16-17, 19)

The passion of this language flows from the very idea of self-sacrifice. You hardly get the idea, here, that the Christian life is designed to bring sure rewards and satisfaction in this life. The language of the New Testament is rarely that of promising satisfaction in this world, but that of strength to overcome in the midst of conflicts and hardships. Nonetheless, the language is powerful, and its sincerity is palpable even at a distance of two millennia:

Do not be surprised, my brothers, if the world hates you. (1 Jn 3:13)

For everyone born of God overcomes the world. This is the victory that has overcome the world, even our faith. (1 Jn 5:4)

And what more shall I say? I do not have time to tell about Gideon, Barak, Samson, Jephthah, David, Samuel and the prophets, who through faith conquered kingdoms, administered justice, and gained what was promised; who shut the mouths of lions, quenched the fury of the flames, and escaped the edge of the sword; whose weakness was turned to strength; and who became powerful in battle and routed foreign armies. . . . Others were tortured and refused to be released, so that they might gain a better resurrection. (Heb 11:32-35)

The writer of Hebrews continues in this vein, recalling passionate suffering, conflict, and striving faithfully against hardships, urging Christians to follow these examples: "Therefore, since we are surrounded by such a great cloud of witnesses, let us throw off everything that hinders and the sin that so easily entangles, and let us run with perseverance the race marked out for us." For, after all, Jesus is our exemplar, who "endured the cross" and endured the opposition of those around him. Remember this, he says, when you think the hardships are too great: "If you are not disciplined (and everyone undergoes discipline), then you are illegitimate children and not true sons" (summary of Heb 12:1-8).

Recently I heard someone comment that people in our day simply want too much. What we need, they suggested, was to moderate our desires. Now that is seemingly a practical idea, and it was an attractive one even to ancient Romans and Greeks. However, the interesting fact is that appetites, ambition, violence and immoderate desires continued unabated—even as they are doing in our day—until the most immoderate of all passions swept over the world in the form of the Christian faith. What was most striking in the personalities of the apostles and the church fathers of the next three centuries, like the prophets before them, could not by any stretch of the imagination be called moderation. In them we find nothing resembling the harmony of vital forces or a calm equilibrium. There are probably no personalities in history less likely to remind you of words like *moderation* and *equilibrium* than the apostle Paul, Tertullian, Athanasius and Jerome. Their imprint on history did not come from balance. It came from passion.

It is true, I think, that their desire for the most ordinary things in life was entirely moderate. Jerome complained that the people of his Italian hometown loved food too much. Athanasius and Tertullian deplored soft living and too many bodily comforts. Most Christian leaders of the early era could be called ascetics. But did this come from a desire to suffer deprivation? Or was it, instead, a result of cultivating the desire for something else—something that they longed for with such all-consuming intensity that these other matters simply didn't count for much?

To answer that question, one needs to understand what the word *passion* means in the context of the Christian life. It is not simply desire. One may choose to call romantic love or even physical desire "passion." And in the language of television drama the word might be used loosely to describe the feelings of a man who is only saying to a woman, "I need you; I cannot live without you," when what he clearly means is "I need you for myself."

That is certainly desire, but is it passion? If it is, then it certainly burns with a very low flame compared to this from *Romeo and Juliet:*

O, she doth teach the torches to burn bright!
It seems she hangs upon the cheek of night
As a rich jewel in an Ethiop's ear—
Beauty too rich for use, for earth too dear!

* * *

Did my heart love till now? Forswear it, sight!

For I ne'er saw true beauty till this night. (act 1, scene 5)

What is the difference in this expression of love? It is simply that it focuses more completely on the object of love instead of the desire of the lover. Unlike so many writers of modern drama, Shakespeare knew the difference between passion and self-interest, and therefore he understood how to give it expression.

The subject need not be confined to romantic love. It is only that the sufferer—the one who is moved by passion most strongly—is the one who focuses mightily upon something outside of himself. Here, for instance, is an expression of passionate intensity about the beauty of music, from Samuel Pepys's diary:

> With my wife to the King's House to see *The Virgin Martyr* and it is mighty pleasant. . . . But that which did please me beyond anything in the whole world was the wind music when the angel comes down, which is so sweet that it ravished me and, indeed, in a word, did wrap up my soul so that it made me really sick, just as I have formerly been when in love with my wife . . . and makes me resolve to practice wind music and made my wife do the like. (27 Feb. 1668)

Here we begin to see what it is, what quality of life, what intensity of longing, that has caused the self-centered and materialistic world begin at times to give way to Christian faith. We have said that it is passion. But what is passion?

The basic meaning is suffering. But by long usage passion carries with it the idea of suffering *for* something or someone of great value to the one who suffers. The notion of suffering in connection with love or desire occurred first of all in theology, in connecting the suffering of Christ on the cross to the love of God. Now it can be applied to a lover who, passionately in love, pursues the loved one with intense feelings and boundless urgency, suffering all kinds of things for the sake of returned affection.

The idea of passion, therefore, usually involves a desire for that which is of great value and rightfully claims one's love. It is a suffering for that which transcends, or goes beyond, the ego. That is why the experience associated with great passion is often referred to as "ecstasy" or "ecstatic"; it is the experience of "standing outside" oneself, of losing oneself in the happiness of the moment, and of escaping the habitual self-preoccupation.

Passion, therefore, describes an experience of great power and attraction. The passionately loving and believing Christians in times when the church made its greatest impact would reinvigorate, shape and direct the moral life of a community. From early Ephesus and Antioch to the England of John Wesley and the America of Jonathan Edwards, the hallmark of spiritual revival and Christian conversion was new moral strength in both the individual and the community. It was evidenced by a power that, as the writer of Hebrews said, "conquered kingdoms, administered justice, and gained what was promised . . . turned [weakness] to strength" (Heb 11:33-34).

What shall we say, however, of growing religious "interests" that, as observers since Will Herberg have noticed, make little difference in the moral life of the community? These interests, as we have seen, revolve circulate around subjects that are decidedly centered in the self. It is not that the growing concern with therapy and with how-to materials (on building self-esteem, managing a budget, finding happiness in marriage, overcoming barriers to success, and so on) do not have a proper place in the church. They do. But when that becomes the whole of religion or a major part of it, then we are focusing on a different direction. And I would like to propose that the word which describes an *excessive* interest in these fragments of the good life is not *passion*.

It is *obsession*.

Obsession describes both the powerlessness of a self-absorbed religion and the final stage of a nontranscendent world view. While passion suggests suffering *for* something, *obsession* also describes a kind of suffering. The term comes from the Latin word meaning siege or blockade. It implies that one so obsessed is cut off from the world; he or she is hemmed in, choked off from the arteries of life. Obsession speaks of a world reduced by inordinate attention to a detail of life, while passion suffers from the sure knowledge that life is too great for the narrow horizon of human experience.

One ennobles life; the other demeans life. One seeks that which is higher than individual life; the other, that which is only part of life. When Jesus sought to fulfill his mission out of love for the Father, we call it his "passion"; when Judas was turned by the prospect of pieces of silver, we call it obsession. When a man is in love with a beautiful woman, we call it passion; when he is in love with her body, we call it obsession. When someone works devotedly for a great cause, laboring day and night for its success, that is passion. When someone does the same to "make a living" or out of ambition, we know it as an obsession.

Passion expends life and finds it. Obsession uses life and loses it. Passion desires life itself; obsession wants only a part of it. Passion sees life whole; through that which it loves it has found the universe. Obsession ignores the universe, so absorbed is it with a fragment of the universe. Passion sees the stars, and having loved them also possesses them. Obsession has spotted something in the mud and does not rest until getting it. Passion opens wide its arms to the world; obsession grasps, like a drowning man grasping after straws.

Above all, passion has to do with a transcendent reality: it desires that which can never be possessed in the literal sense. Obsession is a desire for what is immanent, a desire to close in on a piece of the world. A passion for the transcendent is ultimately a love for God and seeks reconciliation with that which is our source and our destiny. An obsession with the nontranscendent world is ultimately a love for that which feeds the appetite, which quiets the longing for union with the world; it is a search for equilibrium; in so many infinitesimal degrees, it is a desire for death. The difference between passion and obsession is precisely described in Jesus' saying "Whoever finds his life will lose it, and whoever loses his life for my sake will find it" (Mt 10:39). For in losing their lives by being absorbed in a higher longing after God, people engage that for which they exist. And in trying to absorb the pleasures and things of the world that secure only self, by being obsessed with them, their lives are conformed with them in death.

CHAPTER 9

LOVE
WAXES COLD

Needing above all
silence and warmth, we produce
brutal cold and noise.

W. H. Auden

• • •

SOMETIMES ONE INCIDENT—ONE HUMAN STORY—CAUSES PEOPLE TO SEE THE TRUE character of the age in which they live. Such was the case with a story that happened to come out of Italy, but could just as easily have occurred and been told in the United States, Great Britain, Germany or a score of other lands today.

The headline of a *New York Times* story by Clyde Haberman read: "Girl left to wander highway makes Italy examine its soul."

Marco Moretti and his six-year-old daughter Vanessa were driving to the beach, when the thirty-three-year-old father had a fatal heart attack just as they entered a tunnel along the highway leaving Florence. He managed to pull the car over to the side and tell his daughter to make her way home. The six-year-old stepped out into the speeding traffic— six lanes jammed with motorists leaving the city for weekend vacations.

"Cars whizzed by so fast," the story continued, "that the gusts of wind they created repeatedly knocked the little girl down. Scratched, bleeding and in tears, she walked out of the tunnel and along the open highway." For over a mile, and for the next thirty minutes, no one stopped to help her. Finally someone did and phoned the police.

The episode was the talk of Italy the next day, turning up on front pages of newspapers across the country, and for a short time people began to glimpse themselves through the terrified eyes of a little Vanessa. What did she see, emerging from that tunnel, knocked to the ground by the haste of a pleasure-seeking world? Did curious children peer at her from the safety of their parents' speeding automobile? Did drivers, the age of her dying father, stare blankly at the road, trying not to notice? Did a man or woman turn a face toward her, watch her pick herself up off the pavement, see her twisted, anguished face and—most terrifying of all—never change expression? Did anyone laugh? What is sure is that hundreds saw her before anyone helped.

The further question for us is, Can this be what it means to live without hope of heaven? Is a world turned inward upon itself—seeking its happiness within the confines of mortal existence—in truth a world grown finally too adept at self-centeredness to allow for sympathy? Is nontranscendence the opposite of love?

The Decline of Love?
Among the apocalyptic prophesies that we have from the teachings of Jesus in the Synoptic Gospels—wars and rumors of war, earthquakes, persecution, apostasy, and so on—the phrase that ends this catalog of horrors in Matthew has struck me as singularly chilling. It is a summary of all the other aspects of evil when Jesus says, "Because of the increase of wickedness, the love of most will grow cold" (Mt 24:12).

The world of nontranscendence is a world that, more than all else, has abandoned the capacity for love. Many would object that this is too broad and general a judgment to make: other times have been more brutal and less sensitive to pain and inhumanity than our own.

Perhaps that is so. I don't think the idea of the decline of love in a nontranscendent world rests upon counting the incidents of brutality or upon documenting the earnest expressions of humane feeling. But if any doubters are congenial at all to the notion that there is, in fact, a lesser and a greater degree of humane and loving environment in various cultures, and at different times, I would want to ask the following questions:

What centuries, apart from our own, have witnessed the slaughter, the systematic enslavement, the mass starvation of literally millions upon millions for political purposes?

What generation can claim to have produced, within one lifetime, a Hitler, a Stalin, a Mao Tse-tung, an Idi Amin, and a Pol Pot?

How far back in history, prior to World War 2, would one search to find a warring nation that considered it an acceptable prosecution of war to literally destroy an entire city along with a major part of its civilian population? Even Alaric and Attila the Hun had their limits. We would have to go back even further, back to more ancient times, to find examples of total war, since only the twentieth century supplies any recent example.

What other generation has fled *from* the city in order to find safety for their families?

What other generation of professionals in the healing arts has seriously discussed topics such as abortion, euthanasia, infanticide and parricide not as problems, but as possible solutions to problems?

What generation can match the enslavement and slaughter of young and old, men and women, suggested by place names that have become infamous in the twentieth century: Auschwitz, Treblinka, Bergen-Belsen, Kaluga, Archangel, and the whole list of the Gulag Archipelago? Even the fierce religious wars of the seventeenth century, the wholesale child labor and slave trade of the eighteenth century, and the civil wars of the nineteenth century cannot compare.

The Unopposed Will

Are these instances of cruelty and inhumanity only incidentally related to a loss of the sense of transcendence in our age? Or do we have reason to believe that the two sets of phenomena—cruelty and nontranscendence—are connected? Is there, in fact, a predisposition in modern society toward sentiments that perhaps unwittingly contradict the cultivation of such virtues as kindness and love?

I think we can find that modern sentiment is highly attracted to a vision of reality, a kind of theology, that in the final analysis resists these virtues and resists the demands of affection precisely because it resists the idea of otherness or of distinction. In the language of theology the conviction that distinctions are not ultimately valid is called *pantheism*. Alternately it is called *monism*. Let me clarify each of these terms briefly. (For a fuller discussion see the appendix.)

Pantheism speculates that all things are ultimately one. God is all, and all is God; everything is ultimately divine. Or we might say with equal significance, all things are ultimately the same—for when *all* things are divine the implication of a hierarchy of being which "divine" implies is lost.

Monism of any kind, moreover, amounts to the same thing as pantheism. The radical monism of Islam, for instance, invests so much into the sovereignty of the one divine will of God that all other wills become relativized by the one God. And, in fact, all other reality comes into question, because its existence is a mere extension of the eternal oneness of that unopposable will. For this reason the logic of Islam makes possible the interpretation of Sufi mysticism which, in the end, says that God is the *only* reality. The sovereignty and the reality of God are real, while everything else is a manifestation—varied and illusory—of that which is essentially one. Thus the mysticism of Islam comes full circle from declaring the transcendence of a holy and unknowable God to declaring, like Vedanta Hinduism, that all reality is an immanent manifestation of God.

Both pantheism and monism are, in effect, protests against distinction, against a community of persons in whom distinction (and therefore communication) is essential. Monism and pantheism exalt the unopposed will. In modern Western romanticism this manifests itself in an emphasis on will. In Eastern mysticism the emphasis is peace. And in Islam it is power coupled with submission. Monism, in a word, is a vision of the ultimate resolution of things; with barriers eliminated, the "problem" of otherness is resolved in indistinct oneness.

Karl Barth called religious allegiance to monism merely a "glorification of the 'number one.'" "Necessarily, then, we must say that God is absolutely One, but we cannot say that the absolutely one is God." The notion of the supremacy of "the one," Barth goes on to say, tells us absolutely nothing about the character of this one power. Thus the "cosmic forces in whose objectivity it is believed that the unique has been found are varied." And further: "It is only by an act of violence that one of these can be given pre-eminence over the other, so that to-day it is nature, and to-morrow spirit, or to-day fate and to-morrow reason, or to-day desire and to-morrow duty. . . . For all his heavenly divinity each Zeus must constantly be very anxious in face of the existence and arrival of very powerful rivals." He goes on to say that the kind of monotheism found in Islam, where the idea of oneness centers in power and preeminence (not as in Christianity, where the triunity of God also expresses the oneness of love and community), works quite well so long as this conflict over the character of God does not break out. "But," he concludes, "it inevitably will break out again and again."[1]

What are the results on a personal level? If ultimately distinction is invalid, then the barrier between self and the "other"—that which is "not I"—collapses.

One can say, in that case, that I become one with the world. Or one might say that I become one with the divine: my individuality is swallowed up in the divine. But there is an important nuance to this ultimate unity of "me" and the "other." That is, if my experience (or my interpretation of experience) causes me to reject the otherness of reality around me, then I have gone down an altogether different path from, say, that of classic expressions of Christian experience. From John the Apostle to John of the Cross the keynote of life in the Spirit is "love."

Therefore, the true measure of an authentic experience of God is a heightened awareness of the other. In any monist vision, however, it is precisely the otherness of things and persons that is denied. So whether I say that I am one with the world or that the world is one with me makes no difference, tragically, except in the moral life and in the possibility of love.[2]

G. K. Chesterton wrote of a Mrs. Besant who argued that all religions are one and that they all defend the notion that we are really all one person. "If I may put it so," he wrote, "she does not tell us to love our neighbors; she tells us to be our neighbors." Chesterton goes right to the heart of any right-minded objection to the elimination of distinction and to any monist philosophy: "I want to love my neighbor not because he is I, but precisely because he is not I. I want to adore the world, not as one likes a looking-glass, because it is one's self, but as one loves a woman, because she is entirely different."[3]

Recently, in a class called "Introduction to Religious Studies," an enthusiastic student buttonholed me after class and thrust into my hands a book that I had never seen before, but the theme of which looked all too familiar. The title of this little book by J. Krishnamurti is *You Are the World*. The philosophy (if it can be called such) expressed in the book is enormously appealing to an age that has, in various ways, rejected transcendence. Krishnamurti illustrates the fact perfectly that the rejection of transcendence is ultimately the rejection of all distinction, all otherness, all that is not "me." Violence and conflict, he says, proceed from the fact that we accept division and distinction as real:

> Is the "observer," the "me," the "ego," the "thinker," the "experiencer," different from the thing, the experience, the thought, which he observes? . . . As long as there is a division between the "observer" and the "observed" there is conflict.[4]

Conflict, of course, is evidence of the limits of power. Perfect power resolves conflict, which is precisely the temptation that Jesus was presented with when the devil invited him to take on the power of "all the kingdoms of the world" (Mt 4:8). As Oscar Cullmann pointed out, Jesus saw this as the peculiarly Satanic temptation; it was the Zealot ideal, and it was the popular expectation of the Messiah. But it was thoroughly rejected by Jesus with the words: "Away from me, Satan!"[5]

But the unyielding reality of conflict is not, for one given to a non-transcendent analysis, simply the evidence of a not-yet-redeemed world. Rather it is the result of unresolved differences—differences, in other words, that do not take into account the ultimate oneness and sameness of things. And since differences create conflict and conflict is resistance to the unopposed will, distinction itself is seen as a flaw that must be rooted out of both thought and moral life. One could hardly have guessed even twenty years ago, for instance, the energy with which segments of our society would try to obliterate such a fundamental human distinction as the difference between male and female. From the more extreme efforts to avoid gender-specific language to the often hilarious attempts to open every occupation to both male and female on an indiscriminate basis while vainly trying to ignore the elementary physical differences that suit some occupations more to one sex than another, we see the growing obsession with the offending flaw of human distinctions.

No one could justly deny, of course, that sexual, racial and national differences, among others, have often been the occasion for utterly unfair discrimination. But in a world offended by the very idea of distinction, it is not only the unjust treatment of distinct classes that offends; it is the imagined moral failure involved in admitting that the distinction is real in the first place.

Monica Papazu, who came to the West from Romania—at the time a tightly closed communist society—saw this tendency readily through the innocent eyes of one who expected something quite different in the West. In a satire on the life of freedom entitled "Land of Cockaigne," she envisions an imaginary country of frenzied consumption (of goods, of experiences and of people) in pursuit of the desires of an unhindered will.

She prefaced her essay by saying, among other things, "In spite of all that I ought to have learnt, I still remember the feeling they gave me, the feeling that they were afraid of names: a world in which everybody is Dick and Tom and Harry. [A world in which] Dick and Tom and Harry would never introduce themselves by their full names and their surnames, is a world that is afraid of being, afraid of identity, afraid of the potential difference implied by the name."[6]

These fears do not prevail so easily in a world that holds to a vision of transcendence. For, to such a vision, life's essence is found in the possibility and the richness of significant differences, giving rise to relationships among people who are really different from one another and whose differences are enormously interesting. But since these differences can also be felt as a threat, we have with us always the temptation to seek refuge for the threatened ego. This anxiety, as I want to show now, provides much of the motivation for monist or pantheistic philosophies.

"Song of Myself"

Monism can be expressed in collectivism: the sort imagined in Huxley's *Brave New World* or in Lenin's equally imaginative *State and Revolution*. But in the democratic West, the trend toward monism is expressed in a pragmatic individualism. The dream of individualism is that nontranscendent reality will ultimately serve to secure the happiness and satisfaction of the private life. It is founded upon the notion—what amounts in fact to a superstition—that the interests of the individual are not at all compromised by the larger reality. So, in effect, there is nothing to which individuals must subordinate their own needs or desires.

Individuals are, therefore, not a part of a larger whole, as was the case with societies strongly influenced by a transcendent vision. Instead, they imagine themselves as self-created, in a sense, and certainly self-sustaining. "You can be anything you want to be" is what teachers of my era said to their promising students, never suspecting that such a prophecy is finally debilitating. What we become depends to a great degree upon the specifics that have been given into our lives—who we are, where we live, what is our experience and so forth. Individualists, however, prefer to believe that their lives are not a response to the otherness of specific reality, but that reality yields to their individuality. It is as John Donne foresaw: the coherence of society breaks down when "every man alone thinks he hath got to be a Phoenix"—each inventing life over again.[7]

Radical individualism, like monism of any kind, sees the world as resource. The individualist is a pragmatist, which is to say more than that one is impressed by "what works." Because in this pragmatic concern for "what works" there is a hidden prepositional phrase—it is "what works *for me*" that reveals the full meaning of the practical nature. Coleridge, though initially drawn to philosophical pantheism, saw its problematic side in the fact that it finally devolves into self-centeredness. In a satire on the pantheism of Fichte, he wrote:

I of the world's whole Lexicon the root!
Of the whole universe of touch, sound, sight
The genitive and ablative to boot!
The accusative of wrong, the nominative of right,
And in all cases the case absolute![8]

This ego-centered monism that Coleridge parodies here also finds expression in popular attitudes. They are attitudes that resist otherness, and thus resist the everyday implications of a sense of transcendence. In their revealing sociological study entitled *Habits of the Heart*, Robert Bellah and his associates examined the disintegrating effect of American individualism. Possibly an index of the extent to which radical individualism has pervaded American culture is the way commitment in marriage is limited by the overriding concerns for personal fulfillment. In interviews with married couples from the middle class, they found that "on the whole, even the most secure, happily married of our respondents had difficulty when they sought a language in which to articulate their reasons for commitment that went beyond the self." One respondent seemed to "reach for the idea that the interests and indeed the selves of the partners are no longer fully separable in a long-lasting relationship, but his *utilitarian individualist language kept pulling him back*" (emphasis mine).[9]

Perhaps even more disturbing is the fact that those who identify themselves as Christians, which identity should imply something of their sense of self-transcendence, also were hindered by these same cultural biases:

> Similarly, while the evangelical Christians welcomed the idea of sacrifice as an experience of Christian love, many others were uncomfortable with the idea. It was not that they were unwilling to make compromises or sacrifices for their spouses, but they were troubled by the ideal of self-denial the term sacrifice implied. If you really wanted to do something for the person you loved it would not be a sacrifice. Since the only measure of the good is what is good for the self, something that is really a burden to the self cannot be part of love.[10]

Occasionally this inability to understand or articulate interests that go beyond self-interests show up as distinct practical disadvantages. We can see that, for instance, in the frequent contradiction between the American family's "individualistic" philosophy and its need to educate the young.

For instance, statistics show that college students in the United States from Southeast Asian families are outperforming native American students by a substantial margin. This happens notwithstanding the economic advantages of non-Asians and the fact that they have the advantage of operating within their own familiar cultural setting and in their native language. What could be the reason for this? Several inquiries have yielded some insights.

Asian students have a strong sense of obligation to their families to perform well and to justify the sacrifice made by the families. The parents, especially the mother, have given substantial amounts of time to the education and training of their student-children. This has included the mother's staying at home—and thus forgoing additional family income—in order to give attention to educational achievement. This pattern even extended to graduate school, where the mother would often move into the son's or daughter's apartment so she could cook and do household chores, freeing her child for more intense study during preliminary exams or dissertation writing.

This pattern of life becomes possible, of course, where personal sacrifice for the sake of something that transcends self (the family, for instance) appears to be reasonably justified. Where rhetoric, popular philosophy and the habits of society have accustomed us to think that all commitment must ultimately advance one's personal and private happiness, such sacrifice is made to appear frivolous, or perhaps even suspect.

Of course, sacrifice on the basis of obligation (or even love) of a family or nation has its limits. It is ultimately subject to the same error that all nontranscendent loyalties encourage. It is different from self-centeredness only in that the self-interest responds to a corporate identity. It justifies what is good for the group, even if the action may be evil in the context of a larger world or even in reference to the individual. Hitler and Stalin called for self-sacrifice, and in doing so brought untold ruin. A mother can demand loyalty from a child in ways that spoil any possibility of love. And a child can be so demanding of a parent's sacrifice that even the best intentions to help have only served to imprison the child further in self-centeredness.

In a society that has fostered a sense of heaven as its ultimate value, however, something much more thoroughgoing has at least a chance of breaking out here and there. The reason is that a focus on heaven as the goal of life implies that all of existence is essentially a sacrifice. It implies that right action, justice, is not simply good for the individual and not even for the group; but it is good in and of itself. To do right, even at the expense of private needs and desires, is intrinsically good. In a nontranscendent world, actions can only finally be justified on the basis of self-serving motives. That motive may be as simple as "it made me feel good to do that (to do what is right)." But in a world that is convinced that justice—even if it never in this world serves individual interests—is intrinsically right and the very best one can hope for, then no quid pro quo justification is needed.

Not so, however, for the egoistic tendency of pragmatic individualism.

The world, instead, finds its meaning only in the self. The self not only is the center of experience, but must also be the criterion for all value and all hope. Walt Whitman's verses typify the extremity of individualism (and also, along the way, demonstrate the compatibility of pantheism and individualism) with its insistence that personal experience is the touchstone of truth. Whitman cut through reservations about the individualist's rejection of that which is transcendent and (which is the same) that which is nonpragmatic. Instinctively, he knew where the crux of the issue lay. Thus the idea of the "self" as the locus of truth, purpose and value is celebrated in his "Song of Myself."

Whitman at least had the courage to say what few purveyors of pragmatic individualism dare to say: the self is kosmos; it is identified with the world. The world is seen as no more and no less than the extent—the length and breadth—of the isolated soul:

Walt Whitman, a kosmos, of Manhattan the son,
Turbulent, fleshy, sensual, eating, drinking and breeding.

The lines continue with their bombastic claims and comparisons. Without a thought of actually responding to a reality, it makes no difference that it does not illuminate the world, for the world is the self ("I am an acme of things accomplish'd, and I am encloser of things to be"). Therefore the world need not be logical; it is enough for it to respond to the center:

Do I contradict myself?
Very well then I contradict myself.
(I am large, I contain multitudes.)

The self, therefore, is not that which discovers the kosmos, or is limited and disciplined by the kosmos. Instead the self is all impulse; it is primal energy; it is the will unrestricted and unopposed.

I too am not a bit tamed, I too am untranslatable,
I sound my barbaric yawp over the roofs of the world.[11]

The idea steals into individualism, as a type of pantheism, that the self is identified with God. For if God does not transcend self, then the idea of the holiness or otherness of God evaporates in the oblivion of self-worship. For Walt Whitman (who was unabashed enough to say so), "nothing, not God, is greater to one than one's self is."[12]

In "Passage to India," he makes more or less direct reference to the Asian pantheism that he and Emerson so much admired, and he also makes the logic of individualism explicit:

> Swiftly I shrivel at the thought of God,
> At nature and its wonders, Time and Space and Death,
> But that I, turning, call to thee O soul, thou actual Me,
> And lo, thou gently masterest the orbs,
> Thou matest Time, smilest content at Death,
> And fillest, swellest full the vastness of Space[13]

Whitman, to give him due credit, only gives the clearest and most skillful expression to a tendency that existed, in America, alongside other tendencies. It was one that Tocqueville saw as potentially destructive and that Bellah and his associates see working out in a vast disintegration of society before our very eyes. But as a real "habit of the heart," the tendency as Whitman tried to celebrate it is the apotheosis of the self.[14]

The Ethics of Tolerance

Such fundamental convictions as are represented by modern pragmatic individualism do not go unanswered in the actions, the habits and the affections of society. What we find happening as a logical consequence of the individualistic /pantheistic /pragmatic character of modern society are two enormously important changes. One has to do with ethics and the other with the affections—both reflect a shift in the whole axis of human relationships.

The first consequence is that, in a world of mass culture, in which all values become defined only by usefulness to the self, the leading virtue is tolerance.

Remember that the apostle Paul, as well as John, saw love as the supreme virtue.[15] But in a nontranscendent world, loyalty to a different hierarchy of virtues is required. And tolerance becomes the pragmatist's substitute for love.

Tolerance does, in fact, suggest the presence of a positive virtue: it is not love, however, it is humility. Tolerance in religion may suggest the kind of humility that will not presume to know all the answers and is willing to believe that others also have important insights and even superior insights to one's own. Tolerance of those who are distinct in race, nationality, language, sex and so on suggests the humility to admit the irreplaceable value—and the intrinsic value—of those who are different from "my own kind."

The pragmatist, and the individualist like Whitman, however, are not interested in humility. "Nor do I understand," says the poet who sings of himself, "who there can be more wonderful than myself."[16] Instead, he is interested in finding the world shorn of its threat to the ego—its pain and disappointment. For him the world must be a resource. The idea that things and persons have value apart from their use offers enormous problems for the utilitarian vision of the world. It makes for a more pragmatic world to see masses of workers, for instance, as re-placeable parts of a great industrial machine, than as irreplaceable souls each with eternal value.

While tolerance, as an effect of humility, values each thing for its distinction—in other words, for its intrinsic value—tolerance as a pos-itive virtue, and as a moral demand, deplores distinction. It wishes to dissolve distinction and to overcome the separateness that stubbornly refuses to be only an extension of the self. It is the chief virtue of a world without heaven; for just as "heaven is for height and earth is for depth," the idea of tolerance as "positive virtue" resents heights and is offended by depths. Therefore even the attempt to express moral values falls victim to the nontranscendent obsession with leveling and homogeniz-ing all values. "Whatever satisfies souls is true," wrote Whitman.[17] Values are found in the common denominator. It is democracy, all right, but not democracy as a governing expedient but as a metaphysical prin-ciple. It is the conviction that apart from personal preferences things are ultimately the same; nothing has important distinction or value.

That conviction of monism—or of pragmatic individualism—that all things are ultimately the same gives us a clue to the ethical problems that arise. For if nothing is distinct in value, then all things must be settled on the basis of "mere opugnancy" as Shakespeare put it.[18] For justice is reduced to conflict, and conflict to appetite, that "universal wolf" which will at last "eat up himself."

Pragmatism and brute force—that is, the power of use and the use of power—are only distinct in that pragmatism is defined by the subject of the pragmatic purpose. A pragmatic purpose implies, even though it may not be expressed, that a thing or an action is of use to *someone*.

It is an impertinence, of course, to ask who that someone is because nontranscendent pragmatists may be quite indifferent to that question, although the only experience they can really trust—all things being ultimately the same—is their own.

Love and Passion

The second consequence of this privatization of values, or this democratization of values, is the impossibility of love once the conviction of intrinsic value is abandoned. Augustine identified our confused love for that which is of lesser value in the place of those things of greater value as the very essence of the human problem. But if nothing claims love on the basis of its intrinsic worth, then the meaning of love only resides in individual preference.

Things then are valuable because I love them; they are not loved because they are valuable. Apart from the arbitrariness of personal preference, there is (in this view) no reason that anything should claim our love. For all is ultimately the same.

Whitman saw clearly enough the point on which this issue turns, even though his conclusion could only be disappointing. "The most profound theme that can occupy the mind of man," he wrote in 1882, is "the relation between the (radical, democratic) Me, the human identity of understanding, emotions, spirit, etc., on the one side, of and with the (conservative) Not Me, the whole of the material objective universe and laws, with what is behind them in time and space, on the other side."

But he concludes, in agreement with an aspect of Hegelian thought, that the Me and the Not Me ("the impalpable human mind, and concrete Nature") "notwithstanding their duality and separation [are] in centrality and essence one."[19] This only shows that the radical individualist and the pantheist are necessarily in agreement: Whitman at least saw that and followed the argument consistently, much to the chagrin of those radical democratizers who would prefer to hide the seamier side of their philosophy. Both, however, are expressions of monism in moral life, of the tolerance for one reality only—and thus one will. The door is, by force of logic and appetite, open to gross and rapacious egotism.

The Laodicean World of Indifference

The slide into nontranscendence, into monism, tells us that the worst that can happen to relationship is not hatred. The polar opposite of love is not the passionate character of recognizing an enemy as an enemy. (After all, when Jesus says "love your enemy," does he not also declare that there will be enemies to love?) But the opposite of love is dispassion. It is the coldness of indifference.

In his book on the last czar and czarina of Russia, Robert Massie painted a chilling picture of the plunge that the Bolshevik Revolution took beyond the class hatred and social animosity that gave birth to the overthrow of the monarchy.[20] The partisans that first kept guard over the czar and his family had hated the monarchy and all that it stood for—although even in their hatred they were bothered by the fact that Czar Nicholas and his family were, up close, not altogether different from their own families, especially the children. These guards, however, with their revolutionary fervor, their hatred, their remorse and their doubts, were soon replaced by Bolsheviks who had neither hatred nor doubt. And without a trace of animosity toward that royal family, for good political reasons, on an unseasonably cold July morning they shot them every one.

The melancholy principle that works its way throughout a society's attempt to live without pain is that to do so it must live without relationships. Monism, even in its individualistic mode, seems altogether safer but also passionless and cold. Whitman stirred up as much passion as he could while thinking that he went beyond the difference of "the vulgar and the refined, what you call sin and what you call goodness." Yet there is a dullness, a coldness, that overtakes the whole enterprise. E. M. Forster detected this strange, sad weightiness of pantheism that reminded Mrs. Moore, in *A Passage to India*—a title that comes of course from Whitman—of the dull resonance of the Marabar cave.

> The echo in a Marabar cave . . . is entirely devoid of distinction. Whatever is said, the same monotonous noise replies, and quivers up and down the walls until it is absorbed into the roof. "Boum" is the sound as far as the human alphabet can express it, or "bou-oum," or "ou-boum,"—utterly dull. . . . Coming at the moment when she chanced to be fatigued, [the echo] had managed to murmur, "Pathos, piety, courage—they exist, but are identical, and so is filth. Everything exists, nothing has value."[20]

Hatred burns away at what is left of life, but without passion and life, hatred has no meaning. Death, however, has gone beyond hatred; it is the loss of relationship, just as life is relationship pure and simple (for without relationship there is no life). If I live, it is because I relate to the world, to others, and ultimately to God. To resent and reject relationships is to court death and to flee from life. That is why Martin Buber said, "The man who straightforwardly hates is nearer to relation than the man without hate and love."[21]

Now, in a nontranscendent, Laodicean world, we might understand the words "Would that you were cold or hot! So, because you are lukewarm, and neither cold nor hot, I will spew you out of my mouth. For you say, I am rich, I have prospered, and I need nothing; not knowing that you are wretched, pitiable, poor, blind, and naked" (Rev 3:15-17).

CHAPTER 10

EMBLEMS
OF ETERNITY

In this world you will have trouble. But take
heart! I have overcome the world.

John 16:33

•   •   •

IN THE CLASSICAL ERA, GREEKS USED THE TERM COSMOS, OR WORLD, TO SIGNIFY
the unity and wholeness of things. We use the term *universe* in a similar
way. The Hebrews also held to a unifying vision of the world; and they
did so by their insistence on the oneness of God. But when the created
world as distinct from God is mentioned in the Bible, we run into a
habitual expression that embodies a typical Hebrew insight. That is, the
Bible almost always refers to the created order as a dual creation—as
heaven and earth.

There is, of course, a literal sense involved in this expression. The
world is made up of that which is above, the inaccessible sky, with its
stars, the moon and sun, as well as that which is below. In their earliest
forms, these terms *heaven* and *earth* probably refer to the juxtaposition
of the heights and the lower region. But, of course, the dualism of
heaven and earth came to mean more. Heaven also came to represent

the whole idea of a world that is transcendent, the world of angels and of God's indwelling glory. Heaven is not, however, simply God or a figure of speech for God. Heaven is a part of the created order: "God created the heavens and the earth," says Genesis (1:1), and one day there will be a "new heaven and a new earth," according to the Apocalypse (21:1).

The distinction within this created order is of critical importance. There is the earth, that "sphere which is familiar and with which the human being has been entrusted," on one hand. And, on the other, there is heaven, "the sphere of reality which is inaccessible and unknowable" to the human being.[1] So the earth is that which we both receive and employ; and heaven (or the heavens) represents that which can only be received. In other words, the dualism of heaven and earth makes clear that creation is not altogether consigned to pragmatic design. A similar point is made when Augustine said that there are two classes of things: those things that can be used and those things that can be enjoyed— and the higher order of things is those that can only be enjoyed.[2]

The distinction of heaven and earth also means that the world does not find a unity in itself. When considered alone, it is always divided; for its true unity is outside itself in God. Moreover, the lesson that we ought to have learned from our sojourn into materialistic and secular preoccupations is that the more the world is considered apart from God—the more we detach existence from God and attempt to find some other source of unity—the more apparent its fragmentation and conflict become.[3]

Creation, as "heaven and earth," therefore, implies the incompleteness of the world. However, to say that the world does not exist on its own (without heaven) is to say that the mystery of reality that transcends the world is an essential clue to the true nature of the world. The evidences of the world's incompleteness, manifest on every side, constitute emblems of the higher reality that speaks of eternity. The contradictions of nontranscendence that we have given attention to are, therefore, themselves the signs of a greater world, a world of mystery and eternity, where God's will is established, and where therefore the world finds its wholeness and peace.

I will summarize by simply pointing to those emblematic realities that force themselves upon us out of the very contradictions and problems that we have discussed.

Emblem of the Longing Heart: Community, Not Resource

The first sign of a way out of our self-centered, nontranscendent world is, paradoxically, in the very longing of the human heart that reaches such an acute intensity in a materialistic culture. While Christians such as St. Augustine have always seen human longing as a desire that points beyond life, even the nontranscendent world view makes its own perverse witness to that fact. For without a source of transcendence this same hunger for eternity manifests itself in an angry resentment of every limitation, every reminder of the finite, every boundary and every distinction.

That is why there is a bitter and often unreasonable hatred directed against social hierarchy, or any hierarchy of being whatever. Robert Pattison's excellent study of modern rock music, which I mentioned earlier, has pointed out how the various elements of the genre—from the glorification of noise to the gender ambiguity affected by certain performers—are protests against the idea of distinction and rank.[4] The same tendency can be seen in language, where profanity is used as public demonstration that nothing is forbidden, nothing is sacred, everything is common. Reticence in using certain words reflects a society's values, its belief that some things are sacred and are not to be paraded as "profane" in common discourse. But the coarse and common treatment of things that were formally spoken of reluctantly, sparingly and with reverence is a way of protesting the very idea of real values that demand respect. Instead, everything submits to the urgings of the vagrant desires of the individual. With nothing to restrain human will, everything is reduced, in Shakespeare's language, to "mere opugnancy."

However, we must not miss the underlying significance of this nontranscendent protest against rank and distinction, against, in fact, any form of limitation. It speaks of a central urge of the human soul that only finds its satisfaction outside of this world. Its protests against the limitations of form, culture, tradition, manners and even gender are evidences of dissatisfaction with the world. It is a perverse and misdirected protest because it resents the world for not being its heaven. At the same time, however, it witnesses to the boundlessness of human longing for the true heaven.

In some religious thought, the desire for the things of this world is, in itself, a mistake. One must cease grasping. "Now this, monks," said Gautama Buddha, "is the noble truth of the cause of pain: the craving . . . combined with pleasure and lust, finding pleasure here and there, namely craving for passion, the craving for existence, the craving for non-existence."[5]

But in Christianity the fault lies not in the desire but in the misdirection of the desire. The desire itself is ultimately satisfied only in God. One is never satisfied by goods, pleasure and so on, because human desire can be expanded infinitely: it is precisely a desire for God, who alone satisfies those longings. The critical mistake, said Augustine, is in seeking enjoyment in that which is made for our use, and that is intended only to assist us in finding happiness.[6]

Emblem of Wonder: Reverence, Not Pragmatics

While in the university city of Tübingen, Germany, every day I would pass a Marxist bookstore with a huge imposing sign on its roof. The figures of Marx, Lenin and Mao appeared on this sign, alongside the words "Everyone talks about the weather. Not us!"

Now this disclaimer is very interesting. The weather is something that, of course, we can't really do anything about. The bookstore's slogan implies that to spend time talking about things that do not yield to action is out of harmony with an age of science and therefore an age of power. Marx saw the crucial issue when, with his famous eleventh thesis on Feuerbach, he abandoned philosophic contemplation in favor of praxis: "Philosophers have told us in various ways how to understand the world, the point is to change it."

This trend in modern life points out the fact that the loss of transcendence is not simply a metaphysical miscalculation. It is not basically a problem of our theory of the world. It is an intellectual problem only as a by-product of what it is essentially. First, above all, transcendence has to do with that same concern that the prophets of Israel and the saints of the church held to be the primary dislocation in human life: the loss of transcendence is a problem of the affections. It is a disorder of our *love life*.

Science has produced such extraordinary results that we are easily drawn to wish only to be possessed of its power to dominate. That power has never come into view, however, without first passing through the door of contemplation—or of what we might also call "pure science." In reading from the earliest pioneers of modern science we find them often fully aware of the intimate connection between science and the reverent contemplation of nature.

Only a few blocks from that bookstore with its bold Marxist statement stands the five-hundred-year-old Tübingen Collegiate Church, where the early astronomer Kepler set up his first observatory. Kepler was first a philosophy student at the University of Tübingen with intentions of entering the ministry. In the course of his philosophical studies he was introduced to astronomy by Mastlin, who saw astronomy as *principally* the contemplation of the things of God. In the work which Kepler himself considered his magnum opus, *Harmonies of the World*, he ends with a prayer to the "Father of Lights" that reveals his true sense of the inner impulse of the scientist:

> O Thou Who dost by the Light of nature promote in us the desire for the light of grace, that by its means Thou mayest transport us into the light of glory, I give thanks to Thee, O Lord Creator.[7]

Even earlier, Pico della Mirandola saw science as the principal occupation of the human being, who is created in order to "contemplate the organization of the created world, love its beauty, and wonder at its greatness."[8]

Science, therefore, was not *only* a new and seductive power in the world; but it was also (and, in fact, is primarily, even now, by virtue of its dependence on contemplation) a way of coming to know God, the better to place human beings in their proper relation to him and to creation. In this way, science is not merely seen as a servant of the unchecked human will; but it promotes an awareness of the greatness of that which is altogether outside of, and absolutely limits, the human will. In a word, its initial and most lasting possibility is to place within us that which nature always is capable of inspiring: simple, and sometimes terrifying, *awe.*

For the beginning of science is not cold calculation. It is an experience. It is a turning of the soul toward something outside of ourselves, something that creates in us a kind of emotion.

When my brother and I were still rather small, our father used to take us outside into the warm summer nights. Often, at the end of an evening of vigorous play, we would spread out a pallet on the soft St. Augustine grass and talk, staring dreamily at the canopy of bright stars overhead. Usually we would look for meteors, and occasionally we would see one.

"Where do meteors come from?" I recall one conversation beginning. My father explained how stones, perhaps as large as our 1951 Chevy, maybe even as large as a house, wandered in space for years—millions of years, perhaps. Sometimes they were hurtled into space by some great catastrophe thousands of light years away. As we stared toward those heavens, the deep blue of that immense canopy appeared to recede from me, leaving me with a feeling of dizziness. The vastness of space had gripped me, unexpectedly, and I might have described my feeling as something like fear but also, strangely, like a terrible fascination. In fact I knew at that time, though I may have often forgotten since then, that the feeling I had in church when I was really drawn to think about God and the feeling of the ground dropping from beneath me while the vastness of space opened up before me were the same kinds of emotions. Only later, when the feeling was only a memory, would I call one an interest in science and the other an interest in theology.

I often associate that experience with a similar time when, as a teen-ager, I spent a summer afternoon reading Lincoln Barnette's *Dr. Einstein and the Universe*. It was the first time I had read of the mystery of the expanding universe. I learned that many light years away, myriads of galaxies—each as large as or larger than our own—were rushing away from each other, and from a presumed center of the universe, at hundreds of thousands of miles per second. At the outer reaches of the universe these huge systems of stars, planets and other matter were hurtling through space at a speed approaching that of light.

At night fall, out in that Georgia countryside, I looked out at the huge, clear sky with a new sense of wonder. What was I sensing from these discoveries? Was it not the unremitting foreignness of things, the fact that my impact on the vastness of the real world is so entirely negligible? Those stars and galaxies are not part of my world; they are worlds that never gave a thought to me, nor are they the least troubled by my small part of the universe. My only connection with these realities, in any way, is that I may see them and, as Kepler said, that I may join them in the "praise, honor, and glory" of God.

Science that has been lured into the notion of self-important pragmatism may have left behind talking "about the weather," as the Marxists wished to do. Caught up in what "works," people have lost interest in what "is." They have neglected the larger part of reality.

Marxists, or even dyed-in-the-wool capitalists, who have left off talking of weather are in fact saying they have left off wonder for the sake of "doing something about the world." But in saying this, ironically, the world has grown smaller for them, for a small world is the only kind of world that yields to the pragmatic dream. But it's not a world one can live in. Annie Dillard was really expressing the essence of a transcendent world view when she said—in contrast to the self-important sound of that Marxist slogan on the billboard in Tübingen: "There are seven or eight categories of phenomena in the world that are worth talking about, and one of them is the weather."[9]

Emblem of Hope: Faith, Not Obsession

Richard Weaver said that obsession is when a person focuses on something innocuous in order to avoid something painful. The underlying emotion, in such a case, is fear. That is inevitably the underlying emotion of a culture, as we have seen, that finds the fact of human mortality painful, and the thought of a meaningless life unendurable. Rather than contemplate life itself, then, it becomes absorbed in material possessions, fruitless crusades and frantic pleasure-seeking. If it is optimistic, it is unconvincingly so, rather like a condemned man who is hysterically optimistic that the governor will commute his sentence because he cannot face the pain of any other thought. So we have hundreds of good accountants working for good pay at a company the world would probably be better off without; but we have few philosophers and almost no one who reads poetry, much less anyone who writes it. The obsession with the things of the world rises in inverse proportion to the unwillingness to face painful thoughts about life itself.

But what do we fear? It is our own limits that we fear. And that is a fear that arises from not wanting to trust ourselves to a reality that threatens to contradict a self-centered will. But that is also saying that we fear the very fact of otherness, for it is the reality of otherness that sets the limits of self. The reality of the "Not-I" implies that the "I" exists only with boundaries. It also means that the kind of life I live cannot ignore the character of this world of interrelationships, this world of a reality that is over against my self. Christianity goes even farther and says that without those relationships there is no reality, no self, and that to think of self, I can only think in terms of relationship. "Whoever finds his life will lose it, and whoever loses his life for my sake will find it."[10]

This problem, in fact, is what it means to say that our world has lost a sense of the transcendent. We have already seen, in various ways, that a nontranscendent culture is one that has in degrees rejected relationship. Through pragmatic power it attempts to enlarge the sphere of the ego and overcome that which is other than the ego. Or in a monist or pantheist world vision it has simply denied relationship by denying distinction. In either case the nontranscendent culture clings to the ambition of finding a home within the world.

But the hope of heaven, as the New Testament tutored the Christian world in it, is the triumph of relationships. It implies that all things exist for the sake of that which is above and beyond our selfish interests. Heaven is the vision of that which the apostle Paul gives as precept: love as the highest motive and as the very essence of that which lasts forever.[11]

Tradition says that the aged apostle John died at Ephesus. Jerome gives us one version of the story. He said that, on his death bed, John was asked if he had a word for the *ekklesia*. In little more than a whisper he said, "Brethren, love one another." One of those standing near leaned down and asked, "Is there anything more?" The aged eyes, into which the Lord himself had once looked with penetrating compassion, looked toward his questioner. "It is enough," he said, "for that is the Lord's command." John recognized that the whole spirit of the gospel resides in that one command.

A few times in the history of the world, Christians were caught up in the freedom and power of love. And when that happened they were fully aware that something had liberated them to do that which, after all, gave expression to their deepest desires. The promise of heaven was more than anything the assurance that the meaning of all that ever happened to them (and, in fact, all that ever could happen to them) was bound up with the meaning of the universe. Both the image of the cross and the vision of hope in heaven—both the gift to God and the gift of God—meant that they were perfectly free: nothing could ever overcome them. "Whether, therefore, we live or die, we are the Lord's." That is why salvation is so often described as release from bondage, and the gift of the Spirit as liberation.

While the call of the cross leads Christians to look upon the things of God, the call of heaven assures them that God's eye is always upon them. And this glance of perfect mercy is the strength to abide in faithfulness and hope. In Dante's "Paradise," he depicts the presence of

Christ in a final vision of the terrestrial paradise, along with innumerable saints, and the host of angels "which as it soars, contemplates and chants the glory of Him who fills it with love." Dante closes the stanza with the prayer that expresses what many great poets and prophets have recognized as the very meaning of heaven's promise, in this world as well as the world without end:

O threefold light, whose bright radiance, shed in a single beam upon their eyes, doth so content them, look hither upon our storm-tossed lives.[12]

CHAPTER 11

RECOVERING THE HOPE OF HEAVEN

No wisdom is true wisdom unless all
that it decides with prudence, does with
fortitude, disciplines with temperance, and
distributes with justice is directed to that goal
in which God is to be all in all in secure
everlastingness and flawless peace.

Augustine, *The City of God*

• • •

RECENTLY ONE OF MY STUDENTS VISITED THE SHRINE OF V. I. LENIN AT MOSCOW'S
Red Square. Aesthetically, she thought the experience was less than
inspiring. Her expression was "Really spooky."

"But you couldn't have improved on the timing," I said, since we had
just heard that the mortal remains of Lenin—the most famous of all
relics of a secular religion—might be removed to St. Petersburg (no
longer Leningrad) and buried among ordinary mortals, even as the revolutionary empire he founded broke into pieces. This student, and
maybe a few thousand others, would then have been among the last to
visit that famous Soviet shrine.

She described her relief as she emerged from the subterranean mausoleum, bathed in its reddish light, to the open plaza dominated by the onion domes and the brilliant colored spires of St. Basil, one of Christendom's most beautiful cathedrals. Such contrasts! And yet it is a contrast not without meaning. The tomb and the cathedral represent two entirely different visions of the world.

Lenin was the one who wrote to American "comrades" in 1918: "We are invincible, because the world proletarian revolution is invincible."[1] Communism was built and sustained through seventy years, systematically plundering and intimidating the peoples of Europe and Asia, on the strength of a widely accepted myth. Communism believed in its own historical inevitability. Its theorists claimed to hold the future, and that the old order—including the church with its vision of heavenly rewards, architecturally expressed in spires and steeples reaching toward heaven—was destined for the ash-heap of history. Many believed them.

Yet if Lenin is removed from Red Square, his bones with their heavily reconstructed and waxed features will pass on the way to obscurity beneath the soaring spires of St. Basil's.

Memento Mori: Remember You Must Die

What then is the essential difference between these two visions of life—one nontranscendent and the other a vision of hope beyond this world? Does it not consist in this very claim of "invincibility," this denial of limits, and this evasion of the truth of death? Is it not this fear of death and the urgent necessity to find the good of life within this world that drives the frantic search for power, possession and conquests? Under the influence of a terrible necessity to make this life "work," and to make this world serve every need, optimism and a faith in unending progress are seen as moral requirements.

We have seen that this nontranscendent resentment of limits or this outright assumption of no limits is expressed in a number of ways. In its pantheistic expression, it speculates that limits and distinction are really illusory. In its reliance on power, most convincingly demonstrated by the applied sciences, it proposes a world of never-ending conquests, the conquest of time, space, nature and the threats of disease and death. Nontranscendent sentiment relies on evading the reality of limits—it relies on the denial of death, which is the limit of limits.

This denial of death may not be a reasoned defense—in fact, it may even work better when it is not. Reason, after all, convinces us of limits and of mortality. But a certain indignation at the idea of limits can be awakened; and often that, in itself, provides at least momentarily a feeling of moral catharsis, as well as a certain sense of loyalty to nontranscendent ideals. Recently I heard a retired educator begin his address to college graduates by saying, "I am an incurable optimist"—at once proclaiming his virtue, denying the prudent wisdom that stands at the heart of education, and admitting that such an attitude is a kind of disorder. But such sentiments often play well in a generation trained to believe in the world with its inevitable progress and its sure rewards.

In contrast, Christians can acknowledge death realistically, because they have set their sights beyond it. For all the secularist pride in focusing on this life, and not the life beyond, it is precisely because they fail to see life honestly in view of its mortality that they fail to come to grips with life as it really is. Instead of engaging real life, they engage an illusion and operate out of a certain forgetfulness. Denying death, they fail to see life. The ancient motto *memento mori*, "Remember you must die," must be set in contrast to every New Age mysticism that denies death, every utopian dream of earthly perfection and every pantheistic denial of limits.

Titus Dan, a Christian pastor from Romania, told me how his brothers and sisters in Eastern Europe could not help but see American church people as painfully compromised by their materialistic concern for earthly rewards and for immediate victory over all sorts of problems. Under pressure from official communism over so many years, they had been trained by the necessity of choosing between success in this world and living for Christ. And now, even living in an impoverished society, they live materially no worse off than before, but with a life of the spirit as alive, joyful and simple as ever. My friend said, "We really *do* believe a Christian should not love this world."

Under similar difficulties another East European, Vaclav Havel, president of Czechoslovakia, though not a Christian, was moved toward the Christian idea of hope. "Hope is definitely not the same thing as optimism. . . . [The] deepest and most important form of hope, the only one that can keep us above water and urge us to good works, and the only source of the breath-taking dimension of the human spirit and its effects, is something we get, as it were, from 'elsewhere.' "[2]

A New Hope

When we see this essential link between nontranscendence and a philosophy of no limits and when we think how Christian faith acknowledges limits and looks beyond those limits, we can also see before us today the real possibility of hope—hope in its most vigorous form. That is, we have reason to believe that the world is being prepared today, perhaps as never before, to hear the gospel with its message of hope and its vision of heaven.

Let me reflect on this "prognosis," as it relates to an earlier historical experience of the rise of Christian hope.

Death and Resurrection

I was a little dismayed when I first learned that Augustine considered his own age the time of the world's lapse into old age. The spiritual progress of the world had led through the epoch *before* the law (childhood) and the epoch *under* the law (adulthood), and finally to the epoch of grace (old age, *mundus senescens*).

Christians of Augustine's era would have certainly been impressed by the spreading disorders and the rapid decline of culture. The noonday of Roman greatness had long passed. Vandals ransacked the cities of North Africa. In A.D. 410 the unthinkable had occurred with the sack of Rome by Alaric. Confidence in the security of Roman rule would never be the same.

But Augustine had been wrong, it appeared to me at first. The world, after all, recovered from the decline of classical culture, rising to a new emergence of Western culture in the middle ages and then to new heights of science, philosophy and political expansion in the Renaissance. And the modern age has surpassed all previous epochs in the discovery and conquest of the Americas, in escalated wealth and in the rapid accumulation of knowledge and technological and scientific advances—advances which compare with former periods of history in the way a space shuttle compares with an ox-cart, or a computerized printing operation compares with medieval copyists working away on vellum pages. Augustine had seen a world in decline; fifteen centuries later I was looking back on a period of unprecedented energy, discovery and conquest—an age of human advances that far surpassed anything appearing in classical times.

I could clearly detect Augustine's blindness, but I did not yet fully appreciate what he did see. At a time of political crises, the decline of urban life, the conquests of barbarians and the loss of cultural centers, the Christians of Augustine's era became fully acquainted with the reality of a transient world. Even Rome was not eternal.

The facts that they were faced with the decay of a world of ancient glories and that we have lived through a time of expansion and progress on many fronts mean that our perception of the world will be influenced for both good and ill by those trends. Fifth-century Christians were understandably blind to the future; we are perhaps less understandably blind to the past.

What they did see, however, was important for both of our times. Augustine and his disciple Orosius, for example, had to counter the widespread notion that the decline of Rome and the disasters that then afflicted various parts of the world had come as a consequence of Christianity. Augustine argued that such misfortunes do not discredit Christianity, because there has never been a time entirely free of the fortunes and misfortunes of mortal existence. However, such events do prove one important truth: the world is transient; nothing is eternal except God himself and his new heaven and new earth.

The evidence of the world's decay, in other words, gave opportunity for Christians to point men and women beyond the allure of political power and economic security. It was an occasion that begged for an answer to the question: What lasts? What can one depend upon, when the foundations of life seem shattered by blow after blow of misfortune? The fact that political power and the prestige of the Roman Empire had been a powerfully seductive reality must be taken into account. From Augustus (63 B.C.-A.D. 14) on, the security of the "Senate and People of Rome," apotheosized in the *Imperium*, argued convincingly of an earthly order that could not be shaken. It is perhaps no accident, then, that the rise of this new hope embodied in the Christian church found as eloquent arguments in the calamities in Gaul as in the apologies of Tertullian and Irenaeus.[3]

What these things argued for, however, was not beyond everyday and even ancient human experience. That death and decay is the final word for all natural existence was evident then as now. Roman power, nevertheless, offered a straw of optimism to drowning humanity—a corporate optimism. The Christian gospel, however, offered something different from optimism: it offered hope—the resurrection of the dead. The differences between these two are important. Optimism anticipates the best possible outcome based upon present conditions and circumstances. It stands upon the strength of the present and predicts a progressively better future. It meets disasters by rising above them, by believing that the tendency toward improvement is always superior to temporary misfortunes.

Hope, however, is not produced by confidence; it produces confidence. It anticipates triumph in the future because it anticipates help, or grace. Hope meets disasters realistically, expecting that even disaster cannot affect that which is the source of its confidence, but can only strengthen its reliance on that transcendent grace.

Christians alone were capable of meeting the disasters of Augustine's fifth century with a sense of ultimate triumph, because they alone believed in the resurrection of the dead. They alone believed that ultimate good lies beyond the ambiguities and contradictions of this world.

Hysterical Optimism

Now I want to turn back to our own era and say why I think that it, too, is an unusual occasion for the renewal of Christian hope.

Our age also has had its penchant for optimism. Richard Weaver called it a "hysterical optimism." He called it "hysterical," I believe, because the confidence in progress and human improvement had to be maintained in the face of some of the worst disasters in the history of the world. Never have wars embraced so many nations in bloodshed and misery as have those of the twentieth century. Never has the world faced more terrifying machines of war as has our time, with its missile and satellite technology that has rendered land, air and sea bristling with armaments. Since 1945, an entire generation has lived under the threat of a mushroom-shaped cloud.

But we have also been seduced into a particularly virulent form of optimism because our strength over the world around us has never grown more rapidly, nor made more impact on everyday life, nor displayed it power more dramatically and convincingly. Economic and political expansion in the West, and in some nations of the East, has made an enormous impact. The progress of technology has given more reason to believe that progress is a historical necessity. We can well imagine—and for the greater part of two centuries most of us have imagined—that this growth, expansion and progress have no limit.

As many historians in recent years have pointed out, this confidence in progress—this philosophical optimism—is a secular version of the Christian hope.[4] Just as history discloses the redemptive purposes of God and will finally point toward his eternal kingdom, the secular version takes for granted the upward movement of history toward ideals that are vaguely articulated as social justice, economic prosperity or a critical mass of technological skill giving birth to a scientific utopia. Most often, of course, the goal itself is not articulated at all; it is only that the sentiment of an inexorable upward and forward movement of history is the unspoken premise of modern thought. We are either "behind the times" or "ahead of our time"—phrases that would make no sense apart from the modern assumption that the passage of time necessarily means progress. The idea of progress is the "working faith of our civilization," said Christopher Dawson in his book *Progress and Religion*, published in 1929.

The important distinction in the secular version, however, consists in its transferring the achievement of an ultimate good of history from God to those potentialities that exist within the world. Assessing Hans Blumenberg's attempt to distinguish the modern idea of progress from Christian thought, Christopher Lasch says that it is "the assertion that the principle of historical change comes from within history and not from on high and that man can achieve a better life 'by the exertion of his own power' instead of counting on divine grace." Lasch's interpretation of Blumenburg's defense of modern thought precisely locates the place at which "faith in progress" departs from the Christian hope in God's providence.

It also points out the critical lapse in modern sentiment, a small crack in this solid confidence in modern progress through which the light of authentic hope might begin to shine. Lasch has convincingly shown, in his book on "progress and its critics,"

> that "optimism" and "pessimism" remain the favorite categories of political debate [and this] indicates that the theme of progress has not yet played out. In the impending age of limits, however, it sounds increasingly hollow.[5]

This "impending age of limits" brings us back to my thesis. The appearance of limits, the realization of limits, is a necessary prerequisite to a sense of transcendence. And while we speak of a culture undergirded by the self-assured reliance upon progress, we are almost necessarily speaking in the past tense. Observers of late-twentieth-century life speak of this attitude almost nostalgically; we are already past that innocence that characterized so much of the unself-conscious belief in the unfailing triumph of progress.

A *New York World* editorialist could write on January 1, 1901, that his paper was "optimistic enough to believe that the twentieth century . . . will meet and overcome all perils and prove to be the best this steadily improving planet has ever seen." But from that vantage point, on the opening day of the century, he could not have seen the two world wars, the economic disaster of the 1920s and 1930s, followed by the rise of Fascism, the Nazi holocaust, the seventy years of aggressive communist regimes, the threat of nuclear war—all of which have severely tested the notion of a "steadily improving planet" and have finally rendered that notion either ridiculously naive or insensitive to the point of being obscene.

In other words, the "faith in progress" has fallen on hard times. Christians of the late Roman Empire, viewing with alarm the devastation of civil order, found themselves more alert to that which truly offers security. Likewise, in our own time, the tragic revelations that our world is *not* steadily improving may be the signal that people today are ready to turn in a radically different direction.

This signal is especially evident in four modern experiences. They are four areas in which the futility of a nontranscendent vision has become so apparent that we are faced with an unprecedented new longing in the world. People long for an authentic witness to the gospel, to good news that is not simply a variety of the same time-worn confidence in the world of transience. There are four areas where the reality of limits— that indispensable presupposition to transcendence—comes once again into view.

1. *Science and technology* have brought dramatic improvements, but they also have brought us apocalyptic dangers. These two possibilities—a technological utopia and a technological apocalypse—have seemed to appear on the horizon of world history side by side, so that there is no real assurance whether we should greet these advances with hope or with dread. A cartoon in *The New Yorker* expressed the idea precisely and cleverly, depicting the four horsemen of the Apocalypse speeding down a superhighway on motorcycles.

2. *The collapse of communism* has meant the collapse of that ideological system that more than anything else embodied a confidence in progress as inevitable, inexorable, and revolutionary. As Whittaker Chambers revealed in his autobiographical *Witness*, the attraction of communism was the attraction of a religious faith: it was a faith in the vision of a future world with unlimited potentialities. The demise of the communist dream meant, for many people, the end of the hope for a nontranscendent kingdom of heaven.[6]

3. *The violent rise of new nationalistic and racial antipathies* has demonstrated the fragile nature of world peace. Once the Soviet Union weakened its grip on Eastern Europe, an event that followed by thirty or so years the disintegration of European colonial systems, we witnessed (most often with surprise as well as alarm) the reemergence of regional conflicts, ancient national rivalries and racial hatreds among peoples we had almost forgotten existed. It has become apparent that colonial ambitions and the naked power of regimes around the world had merely veiled the reality of these divisions. The tinderbox of regional and racial conflicts only adds to growing anxieties over terrible consequences in a world where a increasing number of nations have almost unlimited capabilities for doing violence to their neighbors.

4. *Environmental catastrophes* and the threat of even greater ecological problems also mark out a limit. The good things delivered by science and technology seem constantly to have a price in terms of their ecological impact. We can no longer think of growth and industrial expansion with the spirit of boosterism common in the 1950s and early 1960s.

We cannot see these things occurring in our times without thinking of the kind of calamities prophesied in the New Testament. Especially in the Synoptic teachings of Jesus, the apocalyptic prophecies include warnings that the stability and predictability of the world will be shaken. These are signs of an age which is giving way to a new kingdom. "Nation will rise against nation, and kingdom against kingdom. There will be earthquakes in various places, and famines. These are the beginning of birth pains" (Mk 13:8).

Likewise, the Revelation centers upon the disasters of warfare, famine, plague and pestilence (Rev 6:1-8, for instance), disclosing the end of the powers of this earth:

> Then the kings of the earth, the princes, the generals, the rich, the mighty, and every slave and every free man hid in caves and among the rocks of the mountains. They called to the mountains and the rocks, "Fall on us and hide us from the face of him who sits on the throne and from the wrath of the Lamb! For the great day of their wrath has come, and who can stand?" (Rev 6:15-17)

The ultimate truth of all the powers of this world is that they will end. Their limits are foreshadowed in the disasters of history, which will culminate in the catastrophic end of the world as we know it. Biblical apocalyptic teachings disclose nothing so clearly as the fact that only in view of the end of all things do we clearly detect the promise of God's eternal reign.

The Restoration of Limits and the Unveiling of Heaven

The apocalyptic teachings also guard against the notion of building a "tower of Babel" in any of its utopian forms. It is a lesson, of course, that we can learn in other ways as well. An essay about evil in *Time* by Lance Morrow spoke the lesson of recent experience succinctly: "Utopia, this century has learned the hard way, usually bears a resemblance to hell."[7]

Albert Camus recognized that the fatal flaw in contemporary thinking was the refusal to recognize limits, and the dream of transcending limits without penalty. The twentieth century fell into the trap of pride. He pointed out that Socrates, "facing the threat of being condemned to death, acknowledged only this one superiority in himself: What he did not know he did not claim to know." Thus, a life of surpassing greatness in those centuries came to its end "on a proud confession of ignorance." Our age has been different, Camus writes:

> We have preferred the power that apes greatness, first Alexander and then the Roman conquerors whom the authors of our textbooks,

through some incomparable vulgarity, teach us to admire. We, too,
have conquered, moved boundaries, mastered heaven and earth. . . .
Alone at last, we end up by ruling over a desert.[8]

Camus's analysis of modern hubris resembles one-half of the classical
Christian view of life. It is the half we have all but forgotten. It is that
we can only see the light of heaven when we are not blinded by the light
of pride.

Humility, Love and the Hope of Heaven

Some of the most thoughtful observers of modern life, then, who see
its dangerous hubris and its mindless optimism, think that the way to
redress the balance lies in the recognition of limits. Camus called passionately for that "higher equilibrium" where human will is bounded by
reason. It was overstepping limits that had brought much madness into
the world, just as ancient philosophers such as Heraclitus had predicted.
"Europe no longer philosophizes by striking a hammer, but by shooting
a cannon."[9]

More recently Christopher Lasch saw that there was a healthy resistance to the excesses of progressive ideology in the lower-middle-class
emphasis on responsibilities of property ownership and the populist
critique of economic development. Even Emerson, that "latterday Calvinist without a Calvinist theology," and those who followed him "reaf-
firmed the ancient folk wisdom according to which overweening desire
invites retribution, the corrective, compensatory force of nemesis."[10]
Lasch points out, moreover, that contemporary warnings against excess
were found in Reinhold Niebuhr's idea of "spiritual discipline against
resentment" and Martin Luther King's nonviolent resistance. "What
these thinkers shared with each other," said Lasch, "and with their
predecessors was a sense of limits."[11]

As a response to modern nontranscendence, this recalling of a "sense
of limits" is important and instructive. But what I would like to say is
that the Christian response—based largely on the teachings of Jesus and
the pattern of his life—is more, infinitely more, than the recognition of

limits. It is quite important to see that the realization of limits is a *prerequisite* to the Christian response. In a way, it is the recognition of limits set in a positive mode. For the Christian, the response to pride is humility, and the object of humility is love.

While humility acknowledges limits, it differs from the mere recognition of limits the way a clear sky at noonday differs from one at midnight. For humility is not only the recognition of human incapacity for doing good, but also the virtue of attributing to God all the good that we possess. "Recognition of limits" is a restraint upon pride, but humility is its replacement. One is negative, the other positive. One cautiously restrains self-will, ambition, greed and lust; the other incautiously loves God and attributes all good things to him. One is a cloudless sky, and the other is sunlight and warmth.

In what sense does humility exceed the mere recognition of limits? Earlier I mentioned that Camus's case against modern hubris resembles one-half of the Christian view of life. The whole of it, of course, is found in one whose life stands far above Socrates' admirable quality of not claiming to know "what he did not know." This was a life that proclaimed in every action and word the desire only to do the will of God. Jesus' prayer at Gethsemane, "Not my will, but yours be done" (Lk 22:42), marks the disposition of his entire life. So while Socrates, on the eve of his execution, nobly refused to claim more than was his, Jesus, on the eve of his execution, placed all things into the hands of his Father. One is admirable restraint; the other, surpassing love.

The apostle Paul expressed the divinity of Christ by saying that he manifested that equality with God, not by self-assertion, but by making "himself nothing, taking the very nature of a servant, being made in human likeness," and humbling himself, becoming "obedient to death—even death on a cross" (Phil 2:6-8).

Jesus' own expression was that "I am among you as one who serves," like a slave who waits on his master's table guests (Lk 22:24-27). His own self-disclosure of God consists in his willing subordination of his authority to that of God the Father. His disciples should rejoice, he tells them in the Gospel of John, because he goes to the Father, "for the Father is greater than I" (Jn 14:28). Therefore, "the world must learn that I love the Father and that I do exactly what my Father has commanded me" (Jn 14:31).

John's Gospel focuses carefully upon this humble desire to claim nothing for himself, but to fully disclose God by obedience to his will. In answer to his critics who objected to his healing on the sabbath, he claimed equality with God, paradoxically, by claiming nothing for himself and identifying his work entirely with that of the Father, because it was obedient work:

> I tell you the truth, the Son can do nothing by himself; he can only do what he sees his Father doing. (Jn 5:19)

It was the kind of confession—at once claiming nothing and claiming everything—that must have thrown his critics into serious consternation. But it was the heart of his self-identity. For his identity consisted precisely in his *not* seeking his own will:

> By myself I can do nothing; I only judge as I hear, and my judgment is just, for I seek not to please myself but him who sent me. (Jn 5:30)

Thus, the Son reveals his identity by virtue of the communication of love in obedience to the Father. The identity of both Father and Son consists in this mutual love and self-giving. God is made known to us in terms of an exchange of life, a mutual attending to an other, a communication between persons. In brief, God is made known in terms of love, for, as John said, "God is love" (1 Jn 4:16). Reality for the Christian does not arise from self-contained individual existence but from relationship and the possibility of love.

It would take us too far afield, perhaps, to take this idea further as it applies to the Christian doctrine of the Trinity. But isn't the idea already implied in the very suggestion of the triunity of God: that God is not simple unity, but knows and expresses his unity in the community of persons, in the mutual indwelling of Father, Son and Holy Spirit?

The incarnate expression of this exchanged and communicating life is the cross of Jesus Christ. When Jesus gives his life in exchange for ours, identifying with our sin and guilt, he discloses the fulfillment of what we see working its way through each action and each teaching in the gospel. In the exchanged life of Christ, we sense already a great power, the unaccountable strength of love. It carries with it the conviction, unarticulated because it is self-evident, that this is the reason for life. And in the resurrection we find God's "Yes"—his fully disclosed promise that a life of love shall not go unanswered by his love.

Sydney Carton, in Dickens's *Tale of Two Cities*, finds himself in the midst of the Parisian Reign of Terror. Eventually he plots to save the life of the husband of the woman with whom he had once fallen in love. He intends doing so by arranging to exchange places with him in prison and, posing as the condemned man, take his place at the guillotine.

Dickens allows us to see the heart of this man who is willing to die for another, and for that man's wife and daughter, when Carton is thinking over the great carnage of a day just past. He recalls the words that were spoken at his own mother's grave when he was a boy. They were the words of Jesus to Martha, "I am the resurrection and the life, saith the Lord: he that believeth in me, though he were dead, yet shall he live: and whosoever liveth and believeth in me shall never die" (Jn 11:25-26). These words set the plot for the exchange of one human life for another in the pages to follow. He thought of these words through the dark night after the execution of "sixty-two" the day before, a night so dark "for a little while it seemed as if Creation were delivered over to Death's dominion." Then he says, "But, the glorious sun, rising, seemed to strike those words." And on the bank of the Seine, he stood "watching an eddy that turned and turned purposeless, until the stream absorbed it, and carried it on to the sea.—'Like me!' "

The power of Dickens's tale depends upon a sense that we each have but can only express when love approaches the exchange of one life for another.

When does that happen? Is it only in the heroic exchange of physical life, such as Dickens envisions? Or is it whenever we find ourselves with the opportunity to cease our endless hunger for attention, approval, self-improvement, gain, power over another, or any lower level of pleasure and, instead, grow in willingness to attend to another, to love another? It is through our love of God and our love of other human beings—and even our proportionate love of the rest of creation—that heaven is realized. For heaven is God's created order in which love is realized and in which self-interest can be laid to rest. It is love of another—that is, exchanging our self-centered life for an other-centered life. It is fulfilling life by loving God and loving one's neighbor. Necessarily, therefore, the apprehension of heaven in the world is never a direct one. That is why speculation about heaven has never yielded much of value in a Christian community or in Christian theology. But the evidences of heaven, the assurance and longing for heaven, come by the steady turning of hearts toward Christ, who is "the way" (Jn 14:3-6) because he is the incarnate reality of God giving his life for us. Then this "darkling plain" of a secularized world will again be warmed by the radiance of love, acts of mercy, words of gentleness, and a new openness of the soul to the goodness of God. These alone, as pure gifts from God, awaken a longing for things above.

APPENDIX

PHILOSOPHIES OF TEMPORAL HAPPINESS

Everything that lives,
Lives not alone, nor for itself.

William Blake

• • •

EVERY READER WILL NOT IMMEDIATELY HAVE AN INTEREST IN LEARNING HOW THIS conflict between heaven-mindedness and worldliness (transcendence and nontranscendence) has been waged in the rarefied atmosphere of philosophy. To many it is a highly interesting part of the story, but it is one I will not insist that all readers give attention to, especially if they have little taste for it. For those who do have an interest, however, I want to suggest how they might begin thinking—and perhaps research-ing further—about this problem as it has played a part in the trends of modern philosophy. The importance of this aspect of the question we have examined along broader lines is that here in the works of philos-ophers and theologians we often find, in concentrated form, an artic-ulation of the way society has collectively come to see the world.

Three Movements against Transcendence

The philosophical question of the loss of transcendence has come to light in three different ways. On the surface these appear to be three entirely different ways of explaining what has happened to secular thought. In fact, as I believe I can show, they are three ways of viewing the same essential movement in modern thought, even though each one concentrates on a distinct result of the movement. The three results of a nontranscendent society that these have in view are (1) the loss of authority, (2) the hatred of distinction and (3) the apotheosis of power.

These three results actually give us a good summary of the kinds of destructive winds that blow through a culture that has rejected its vision of transcendence. What I say here will only be a brief overview. For any one of these approaches to the question, the works I cite will yield a much more complete treatment of the question involved. My purpose here, however, is to show that on every side we are dealing with the same problems and the same questions—questions to which the Christian hope of heaven gives an enormously satisfying answer. It is an answer that meets the human need in terms of intellect, but also in terms of the affections: what we love and what we value. Yet because it is an answer that requires surrendering to the facts of human finitude and moral liability, the modern spirit has typically rebelled in these three predictable ways: against authority, against the limits of self (distinction) and against the limits of will.

The Decline of Logical Realism

Richard Weaver of the University of Chicago has perhaps made the liveliest and most far-reaching case for seeing the cultural decline of the West as being strongly tied to the nominalist-realist controversy of the late fourteenth century. He proposed that the widening circles of disorder in Western life can be traced back to a philosophical choice to abandon the idea that universals have a reality that is independent of, and higher than, the particular existence of things. "Have we forgotten our encounter with the witches on the Heath?" he asks, referring to the scene in *Macbeth* where an evil choice was made. "What the witches said to the protagonist of this drama was that man could realize himself more fully if he would only abandon his belief in the existence of transcendentals."[1]

The realists in this controversy, such as John Scotus Erigena and Anselm of Laon, held to the idea that general and abstract categories of things are real, whereas particular things were examples that manifest reality. For example, the idea of a tree and the reality of a particular pine tree do not exist on the same level. Particulars come and go—they are only the temporal manifestation of something that is lasting and does not come into existence and disappear from existence.

The emerging nominalist position, however, insisted that the idea of a tree rises from the particular and concrete existence of trees, to which we assign names. The nominalist assertion, notwithstanding its common designation, runs deeper than the phenomenon of language. It is not simply the idea of giving names to things that is implied. It is that the *concept* of the world, the vision of the world—including categories, names, principles, virtues, and so on—are generated by the human imagination and projected upon a reality that only consists of the concrete and particular things.

Now I must admit, however, that to state this controversy in such stark contrasts is not entirely fair. There was not *a* nominalist position. But there were a number of nominalist systems that ranged along a scale from moderate to radical. And though nominalism stated in such stark terms may sound like a preamble to materialism, it certainly was not the case in the minds of its earliest proponents. William of Occam, in England, and Gabriel Biel, in Germany, were leading intellectuals in this revolution in the world view. But they were also leading Christian thinkers who believed deeply in a transcendent reality. It was a long time before the full implications of a nominalist position would appear in discussions among intellectuals, and even longer before the impact of such thought weighed heavily in ordinary public life and discourse.

But it was, as Weaver points out, the first faint shadow of something ominous that was to bring about a change in the Christian concept of reality. The issue that comes to light, however, is of huge importance in the ordering of human life. The issue is no less than whether there is a source of truth higher than, and independent of, humankind. As Weaver pointed out: "The practical result of nominalist philosophy is to banish the reality which is perceived by the intellect and to posit as reality that which is perceived by the senses." Thus, "the question of what the world was made for now becomes meaningless because the asking of it presupposes something prior to nature in the order of existents."[2]

Among the results of this intellectual change stands one of central importance. The articulation of values implies an abstract ordering of things. One action is seen as more virtuous than another. One thing is more valuable than another. One mode of art is sublime; another is worthless and ugly. One boy knows his mathematics, another needs improvement, and a third has failed. The sluggard is foolish, and the industrious is wise. We cannot speak of human action, social order, justice, beauty or virtue without implying a hierarchy. The moment we attempt to pretend that everything is on the same level and that evaluation is impossible, we find ourselves caught up in every possible contradiction. Because the truth is that we *do* imply that one action is preferable to another and that one thing is of greater value than another, whether we wish to do so or not. Otherwise, all things and all actions are meaningless, and the most sensible thing (You see! There *I* did it— "most sensible") is to lapse into silence.

But the point raised by the trend toward nominalism is whether, in fact, these hierarchies of value have any intrinsic meaning, or whether they are actually arbitrary constructions of the human will. Are these generalities and abstractions of value rooted in some reality apart from the world of particulars, or are they simply projected upon the world as human conventions? It is the tendency of nominalism to convince us that such evaluations are arbitrary and are imposed upon a world of undifferentiated particulars.

The moral confusion this state of mind *could* cause is obvious. (It is with some indebtedness to the human being's stubborn attachment to reality that the full implications of this thinking seldom appears.) For example, last year I was involved in a panel discussion on the topic of ethics and the evironmental crisis. The speaker before me on the program tried to base his argument against human exploitation of nature on the notion that, as he said, "human beings have no more right to live than bears." This is a popular and modern theme, and I imagine that the audience and the media responded to it favorably.

But I thought that it was also a seriously wrong-headed approach to saving the environment. Granted, bears have a value, one that even transcends their value to humanity. However, as I tried to show, if everything is of equal value, then there is no hierarchy of values to appeal to when one is trying to save the bear. And if one thing in nature is not inherently more important than another, then the question of the survival of one species or another (for example, whether bears are not of more service as bear rugs) becomes a question that can only be resolved on the level of power and conflict.

The Apotheosis of Power

A second attempt at ordering life without transcendence is by appeal to power. The automobile in front of me this afternoon displayed a bumper sticker that read, "We'll get along fine as long as you realize I'm God." The joke—if that is what it is—lacks the subtlety that would make it funny, but it does point out a certain popular concept of God.

God is, in a word, someone who gets his way. Now that is a long way from the Aristotelian idea of a God of monadic power; but it is even further from the Christian and Hebrew idea of a God of self-giving love. There is something present in modern thought, however, as Jürgen Moltmann has pointed out, that identifies God with simple, direct, coercive power. And in the same way that theologians identify God with power, the world at large has been drawn to a worship of power.

This *apotheosis of power*, as I have called it, has brought on what Moltmann calls the "crisis of domination." In terms of the ecological crisis, he says that human beings have learned that their proper relationship to nature is one of domination and exploitation.

Where did this originate? Some would say it comes from the Bible where the Genesis creation story tells us that humankind was given dominion over all that God has placed on earth. Moltmann denies that this is the source. In the first place, the idea of dominion in the Old Testament involves the idea of *protection* as well as *ordering*, and it was only at a much later date that the role of humanity was seen as that of exploiter, as one who uses power for the purpose of domination, and to serve selfish ends.[3]

Instead, he says, we see this notion arising about four hundred years ago.

With the coming of greater and greater possibilities in the realm of science and technology, Moltmann explains, there was also a tendency to see God's preeminent attribute as *potentia absoluta*—absolute power:

> Power became the foremost predicate of deity, not goodness and truth. But how can the human being acquire power, so that he may resemble his God? Through science and technology; for "knowledge is power," as Francis Bacon exultantly proclaimed.[4]

Of enormous influence in the emerging experience of science was the thinking of René Descartes. In his *Discours de la méthode*, he states that the aim of science (that is, of knowledge) was to make men "masters and possessors of nature."[5] Thus nature becomes an object to be analyzed, not to be contemplated for its own sake, but to determine how it might yield to human purposes and designs. The object of science comes to be "divide and conquer." Thus human beings live not as members of a created order, in community with nature, though in a unique role. Instead they come as its lord and owner. Science becomes the instrument by which this relationship is made possible, if not in fact, at least to the imagination. For that reason the vision that has dominated so much of the past four centuries—encouraged by the undeniably spectacular gains in science and technology—has been one of humanity dominating nature.

Having endured a major hurricane not long ago, I can tell you that there are experiences that take the edge off that vision of being "master and possessor of nature." Nevertheless, that is a prevailing idea, and it is one that exalts the value of power.

The scientific ideal, with its attendant notion of "knowledge is power," is not confined, of course, to the natural sciences. Auguste Comte envisioned the potential of science as a basis for a new society. Karl Marx envisioned scientific socialism. Freud wished his psychoanalysis to be seen as a science, with some effective power in the realm of the psyche. War has increasingly become a contest of technologies. Businesses, bureaucracies and churches depend upon the analysis of society, made believable by reams of computerized data—all giving the impression (whether or not it is more or less illusory) that the possessors of such knowledge stand in a power relationship to the populations they wish to influence.

The difficulty with such a relationship, and such a vision, is that it implies the exertion of the will over something or someone. That "thing," so moved by the will, becomes no longer a subject with which one enjoys companionable mutual relationship. "It" becomes an object. And the more perfectly an object obeys the will, the more it becomes a mere extension of the self. Relationship requires otherness. Power overcomes otherness and eliminates relationship.

Students of the New Testament will recall that Jesus is one who resisted the use of power to accomplish his purpose. That offer to exercise power—as Messiah or King—was seen as the peculiarly Satanic temptation (Mt 4:8-10; 16:21-23).

In the New Testament, more than anywhere else, we see power as, in the first instance, a destroyer. Service, suffering and love imply respecting the *subject*, the otherness, the "Thou" (as Martin Buber expressed it) in the ones to whom we relate.

Thus Paul described the husband's role as "head of the wife" precisely as "Christ is head of the church." This means that he sacrifices self-interest for her, imitating Christ who "loved the church and gave himself up for her" (Eph 5:25). And Jesus told his disciples not to follow the example of the Gentiles whose rulers "lord it over them, and . . . exercise authority over them" (Mt 20:25). Instead, if any would be great, they must serve the rest. That was in Jesus' teaching the nature of the kingdom. It was, in fact, the nature of life itself, because power, though necessary within limits, has an inevitable quality—it destroys.

A pediatrician I know, Dr. Ed West, is widely appreciated for his lectures on child rearing. The parent, he points out, has two important assets from the beginning of the child's life. (1) Obviously, the parent is bigger and stronger than the child, so the mother or father can, and must, force the child to do the parent's will. (2) However, the second important asset is that the child wants the parent—and this asset is easily transformed into wanting to please the parent. The doctor goes on to explain that the object of child rearing is to bring the child to the point where he of she "goes the right way" as a result of free will. Often—and if things go well, less and less often—the parent resorts to the use of size and might to force the child to "go the right way."

However—and here is a major point of parental wisdom—the parent must recognize that employed force is always at the expense of the second asset. The child's natural attraction to the parent is diminished to the extent that the parent must use force. It creates a barrier of resentment. It is perhaps only temporary, but it is there. So the point Dr. West makes is, Use this remedy when necessary, but remember it is expensive medicine. Power always diminishes relationships. This lesson applies to all areas of life: domination destroys, love makes alive. In a fallen world, one cannot exist without the other. Love is given a space in which to grow only where law, domination and force impose a certain order. But power must always be seen as the means (and a costly means at that) and not an end.

The Hatred of Distinction

A third philosophical fashion, which in a way summarizes the other two and which has an enormous bearing on modern life, is properly called pantheism. If nominalism promises relief from metaphysical absolutes, and power provides freedom from circumstances that frustrate the will, then pantheism combines the promise of toppling absolutes and dissolving individual limits.

To the popular mind, pantheism relates to Eastern religions and to the Western adoption of Vedanta Hinduism. Pantheism simply means, however, an identification of the world with God: the "all" of the world is God and God is all. A case can be made that philosophical pantheism has played as large a role in Western thought as it ever did in the East. While Hinduism is often described as pantheistic, one will seldom find that form of philosophic Hinduism in practice in Indian communities.

In the West, by contrast, beginning with pre-Socratic Greek philosophy, one can find in pantheism a constant possibility among the range of philosophic and theological options. And in many instances it has been among the strongest intellectual influences in society. Such was the case, for instance, during the several centuries (from about the third century B.C. until the rise of Christianity) that the Stoic philosophy filled the vacuum left by religious cynicism and skepticism in the Greco-Roman world. As Robert Pattison has pointed out, "Pantheism is as old as philosophy, and every age has had its believers."[6] From El Hallaj, of the Islamic Sufis, to William Blake in the Christian tradition, there has from every religious camp emerged the possibility of a pantheistic vision of reality.[7]

Aristotle assumed that Xenophanes' (c. 570-480 B.C.) idea of God included his quality of being coextensive with the universe—what we would call pantheism. Melissus of Samos (c. 450 B.C.) was certainly a pantheistic philosopher. So was Heraclitus (c. 536-470 B.C.), who thought that all opposites are absorbed into a cosmic whole: "Things taken together are whole and not whole . . . out of all there comes a unity, and out of unity all things."[8] Naturally, then, the theological conclusion is that "God is day night, winter summer, war peace, satiety hunger"—he is the dissolution of opposites, the end of distinction, the abolition of limits.[9]

It seems that pantheism is not a particular religious system of belief; it is rather a theoretical tendency any time a religion begins to reach beyond the grossly material, the particular and the provincial expression, to one of universal and, therefore, more abstract concepts. Thus the religion of the Indus Valley, Hinduism, became pantheistic only when it emerged from its mythic expression to the more theoretical attempts at a universal wisdom in the Upanishads and in what is called *Vedanta* (meaning "end of the Vedas") Hinduism in the first century B.C. Stoicism, a Western pantheism, gradually replaced the declining polytheistic Greco-Roman religions under the reforming influence of philosophy. It seems that any time there is an attempt to reconcile the world of multiple "things" with the unity and oneness of the world, there is the option of short-circuiting that difficulty by declaring the multiplicity as maya, or illusion. The temptation to resolve the question in this manner, however, is no more Eastern than it is Western. It has made its appearance in every society of advanced culture with a highly developed need for abstract thought.

The only reason such a tendency feels alien in the West is that theism—in the form of Christianity, Judaism and Islam—have so long resisted the pantheistic alternative. For several reasons, theists have detected a grave threat to their understanding of God and their understanding of human life in the pantheistic alternative. They have accurately sensed that a faith which relies upon the kind of discipline (in moral and devotional life) that calls for self-giving love cannot long endure where distinctions are seen ultimately as illusions.

The Pain of Life and the "Happiness" of Death
In these three modern trends—the rejection of absolutes in nominalism, the pursuit of power in science, and the loss of distinction in pantheism—we have three trends that are, in effect, aspects of the same trend. Each of these appeals, in a certain way, to what I will call the "imperialistic self." They respond to a metaphysical threat, one that every human being suffers in one way or another. This metaphysical threat is directed

against the self. It says, in effect, "You are limited, you are finite." You are limited, first of all, by the *otherness* of existence, other persons, other things. These are not simply extensions of your own self-consciousness, but they exist apart from you and without regard to you. Moreover, the fact of death is the final irrefutable statement of human finitude; it is its ultimate expression and the final insult to the self that imagines itself the center from which all reality radiates.

An aspect of that metaphysical insult is that the individual and society must respond to an outside reality. The world will not yield to the vagrant wishes and vain desires of the human being. The development since the Renaissance in rejecting realism (by the rise of nominalism) has increasingly allowed us to believe there are no absolutes. It has promoted the notion that society yields to the unfettered imagination, that only freedom is absolute.

Thus the assurance, via nominalism, that there are no transcendentals, no universals, no absolutes, comes as a relief. The imperial self imagines it is free from moral contradictions and thus from guilt. Science, likewise, can be imagined as the source of unlimited domination in the physical realm. And pantheism takes away the fear of God: for if the boundary between me and God has been repealed, then who is to say whether I have been taken up into God, or God has been taken up into me?

Only heaven can prevent theology from becoming psychology.

Notes

Chapter 1: The Eclipse of Heaven

[1]*Newsweek*, 27 March 1989, p. 53. Jan Kerkhofs, "Good Heavens," *Concilium* 123 (1979):1-12.

[2]Some estimates run as high as 30,000; see, for example, "Lisbon" in *The New Encyclopedia Britannica* (Chicago: Encyclopaedia Britannica, 1989), 23:81.

[3]T. D. Kendrick, *The Lisbon Earthquake* (Philadelphia: Lippincott, 1957), p. 137.

[4]Antonio do Sacramento, cited in Kendrick, *The Lisbon Earthquake*, pp. 126-27.

[5]Kendrick, *Lisbon Earthquake*, p. 211 (a translation).

[6]"Heaven," *Newsweek*, 27 March 1989, p. 53.

[7]P. T. Forsyth, *Positive Preaching and the Modern Mind* (Grand Rapids, Mich.: Eerdmans, 1964), p. 32.

Chapter 2: The Church's Failing Vision

[1]John Baillie, *And the Life Everlasting* (London: Oxford University Press, 1936), p. 15.

[2]Alan Richardson and John Bowden, eds., *The Westminster Dictionary of Christian Theology* (Philadelphia: Westminster Press, 1984), p. 146.

[3]This passage, originally from the *Alabama Book of Legal Forms*, is used most widely because of its inclusion in J. R. Hobbs, *The Pastor's Manual* (Nashville: Broadman, 1934), one of the most popular Baptist manuals in this century, having gone through thirty-six printings by 1970 and today still in print.

[4]In fact, I hope it is already apparent that the term "over us" is not intended in any astrophysical sense. I might as well say "outside," or "inside," if spatial relations were the only important thing conveyed in the idea of a heaven over us.

But if we mean by heaven a reality that supersedes and is exalted above every temporal thing, that creates a hierarchy of value in the world, that is more than a succession to this life (else "outside" would do as well), and that is also something different from the world (else "inside" would be preferable), then the traditional language is not easily replaced. It is a reality "over us" in that it is the greater reality, the ultimate value, the final purpose and the consummation of all things.

[5]Matthew Arnold, "Dover Beach."

Chapter 3: The Bright Shadow of Heaven

[1]Jaroslav Pelikan, *The Excellent Empire* (San Francisco: Harper, 1990), p. 41.

[2]Athanasius, "On the Incarnation of the Word," trans. Archibald Robertson, from *Christology of the Later Fathers*, ed. Edward Hardy (Philadelphia: Westminster Press, 1954), pp. 81-82.

[3]Athanasius, "Incarnation of the Word," p. 83.

[4]Ibid.

[5]Jaroslav Pelikan, *The Shape of Death* (London: Macmillan, 1963), p. 27.

[6]Ibid.

[7]Athanasius, "Incarnation of the Word," p. 85.

[8]Edward Gibbon, *Decline and Fall of the Roman Empire* (London: J. M. Dent & Sons, 1960), 15(2):453.

[9]Ibid.

[10]Marsha Spradlin, *Transformed One Winter* (Nashville: Broadman, 1989), p. 165.

[11]Jan Kerkhofs, "Good Heavens," *Concilium* 123 (1979):1-12.

[12]Helen Oppenheimer, *The Hope of Heaven* (Cambridge, Mass.: Lowley, 1988) p. 148.

[13]Augustine, *Commentary on John*, 12:11, in *Nicene and Post-Nicene Fathers*, ed. Philip Schaff (Grand Rapids, Mich.: Eerdmans, 1986), 7:85.

[14]Jürgen Moltmann helpfully uses this expression in *The Trinity and the Kingdom* (San Francisco: Harper & Row, 1981), pp. 174-78, and other places. He also follows John of Damascus in referring to this unity linked with community as the *perichoretic* unity of Father, Son and Holy Spirit.

Chapter 4: At Home in the World

[1]John Calvin, on Hebrews 11:1, in Jürgen Moltmann, *Theology of Hope* (New York: Harper & Row, 1967), p. 19.

[2]St. Gregory of Nyssa, *The Life of Moses*, Classics of Western Spirituality (Mahwah, N.J.: Paulist Press), p. 39.

[3]George Bernard Shaw, *Man and Superman*, act three, in *Plays by George Bernard Shaw* (New York: Signet Classics, 1960), p. 341.

[4]*The Ecclesiastical History of Eusebius Pamphilus*, trans. Christian Frederick Cruse (Grand Rapids, Mich.: Baker Book House, 1979), p. 219.

[5]Ibid., p. 218.

[6]Ibid., p. 220.

[7]Charles Kingsley's preface to *Hypatia* (New York: Caldwell), pp. 1-2.

[8]*Eusebius Pamphilus*, p. 176.

[9]*Epistle to Diognetus*, in F. F. Bruce, *The Spreading Flame* (Grand Rapids, Mich.: Eerdmans, 1958), p. 177.

[10]Cited in Eric O. Springstead, *Simone Weil and the Suffering of Love* (Cambridge, Mass.: Cowley, 1986), p. 125.

[11]Ninian Smart, *The Religious Experience*, 4th ed. (New York: Macmillan, 1991), p. 176.

Chapter 5: Self-Transcendence

[1]Cf. Mircea Eliade, *Patterns in Comparative Religion* (New York: Meridian, 1963), pp. 379-80.

[2]R. Albert Mohler, "I'm OK, You're Codependent," *The Christian Index* 169, no. 22 (31 May 1990):2.

Chapter 6: Community as Human Resource

[1]Lewis Carroll, *Alice's Adventures in Wonderland* (New York: Knopf, 1983), p. 72.

[2]Delivered in a paper entitled "Ecological Crisis and the Consumer Society," at a Midwest regional meeting of the American Academy of Religion, Spring, 1987; later published in *God, Hope and History* (Macon, Ga.: Mercer University Press, 1988), p. 178.

[3]*God, Hope and History*, p. 179.

[4]Aleksandr Solzhenitsyn, *The Gulag Archipelago* (New York: Harper & Row, 1979), 3:92.

[5]This discussion was published in Helmut Thielicke, *Between Heaven and Earth* (New York: Harper & Row, 1965), p. 147.

[6]Ibid., p. 161.

[7]Ibid., pp. 163-64.

[8]Albert H. Keller, Jr., "Prolonging Life Can Give It a False Value," *The News and Courier* (Charleston, S.C.), 21 July 1990.

[9]C. Everett Koop, "The Slide to Auschwitz," an afterword to Ronald Reagan et al., *Abortion and the Conscience of the Nation* (Nashville: Thomas Nelson, 1984), p. 48.

[10]Reagan et al, pp. 79-82.

[11]John Wesley, *A Plain Account of Christian Perfection* (London: Epworth,

1976), p. 22.

12Sigmund Freud, "New Introductory Lectures on Psycho-Analysis," in *Great Books of the Western World* (Chicago: Britannica, 1952), 54:874-75. Freud stated that the three forces that contend with his psychotherapy by disputing the position of science are art, philosophy and religion. "Of the three forces," he said, "religion alone is a really serious enemy." It is significant that all three of these depend upon a sense of the transcendent.

13Ibid., p. 878.

14Ibid., p. 884.

15Cited in Richard M. Weaver, *Ideas Have Consequences* (Chicago: University of Chicago Press, 1948), p. 118.

Chapter 7: Science as Pragmatics

1David L. Edwards, ed., *The Honest to God Debate* (Philadelphia: Westminster Press, 1963), pp. 270-71.

2This question, once posed by Bertrand de Jouvenal, was related to me in 1986 by Professor Jürgen Moltmann. It happens to be, also, a restatement of the dilemma of power that M. de Jouvenal expresses in *On Power: Its Nature and the History of Its Growth,* trans. J. F. Huntington (Boston: Beacon Press, 1945).

3Allen Tate, *Essays of Four Decades* (Chicago: Swallow Press, 1968), p. 6.

4Allan Bloom, *The Closing of the American Mind* (New York: Simon & Schuster, 1987), pp. 339-40.

5Quoted in "Philosophical Schools and Doctrines," *Encyclopedia Britannica,* 15th ed., 25:647.

6John Herman Randall, Jr., "Dualism in Metaphysics," *Essays in Honor of John Dewey* (New York: Octagon Books, 1970), p. 315.

7See an excellent study of this reverence for progress in Christopher Lasch's *The True and Only Heaven* (New York: W. W. Norton, 1991).

8Randall, *Essays,* p. 315.

9Jürgen Moltman, *God in Creation* (New York: Harper & Row, 1985), p. 28.

10Aldous Huxley, *Brave New World* (London: Grafton Books, 1977), p. 46.

11Ibid., pp. 143-44.

Chapter 8: Religion as Obsession

1Henry A. Van Dusen, "Theological Standards Today," *Union Seminary Quarterly,* March 1959, p. 31.

2Will Herberg, *Faith Enacted as History* (Philadelphia: Westminister Press, 1976), pp. 259ff.

[3]Robert Pattison, *The Triumph of Vulgarity* (New York: Oxford University Press, 1987), p. 186.

Chapter 9: Love Waxes Cold

[1]Karl Barth, *The Doctrine of Reconciliation: Church Dogmatics,* vol. 2, pt. 1, ed. G. W. Bromily and T. V. Torrance (Edinburgh: T. & T. Clark, 1956) pp. 448-49.

[2]An important study of this distinction in religious experience, one that illustrates this point in terms of the recognition of the "other," is R. C. Zaehner's *Mysticism: Sacred and Profane* (Oxford, 1961).

[3]G. K. Chesterton, *Orthodoxy* (Garden City, New York: Image, 1959), p. 131.

[4]J. Krishnamurti, *You Are the World* (New York: Harper & Row, 1972), pp. 5-6.

[5]See Oscar Cullmann, *Jesus and the Revolutionaries* (New York: Harper & Row, 1970), pp. 38-40.

[6]Monica Papazu, "Submitted to Freedom," *Christian Scholars Review* (1990) 19:4; pp. 407-417.

[7]John Donne, "An Anatomie of the World: The First Anniversary," in *The Complete Poetry of John Donne,* ed. Charles Coffin (New York: Modern Library/Random House, 1952), p. 191.

[8]Cited by Pattison, *The Triumph of Vulgarity,* p. 25.

[9]Robert Bellah et al., *Habits of the Heart* (Berkeley: University of California Press, 1985), p. 109.

[10]Ibid.

[11]Walt Whitman, "Leaves of Grass," in *Complete Poetry and Selected Prose,* ed. Emory Holloway (London: Nonesuch, 1967).

[12]Whitman, "Song of Myself," in *Complete Poetry and Selected Prose.*

[13]Whitman, "Passage to India," in *Complete Poetry and Selected Prose.*

[14]Obsessions, especially someone else's, are notoriously difficult to celebrate. They might be interesting in a morbid sense. It is instructive that a certain dullness and torpor pervades Whitman's poetry in spite of his evident power of expressive and evocative images and his seldom surpassed poetic skill. It is not his lack of ability that makes it so; it is the impossibility of elevating "self" to the level of universal attraction. Only that which transcends self can communicate passion, i.e. love.

[15]1 Corinthians 13 and 1 John 4:7-12 are examples.

[16]Whitman, "Song of Myself," stanza 48.

[17]Whitman, "Song of Prudence," in *Complete Poetry and Selected Prose.*

[18]William Shakespeare, *Troilus and Cressida,* act 1, scene 3, in *Shakespeare: The Complete Works,* ed. G. B. Harrison (New York: Harcourt, Brace &

World, 1968), p. 983.

19Whitman, *Complete Poetry and Selected Prose*, p. 786.

20Robert K. Massie, *Nicholas and Alexandra* (New York: Atheneum, 1967), pp. 515-17.

21E. M. Forster's, *A Passage to India* is cited here and discussed in reference to modern rock music culture in Pattison's *The Triumph of Vulgarity*, p. 72.

22Martin Buber, *I and Thou* (New York: Macmillan, 1958), p. 6.

Chapter 10: Emblems of Eternity

1Jürgen Moltmann, *God in Creation* (New York: Harper & Row, 1985), p. 159.

2*On Christian Doctrine* I.3, in *Great Books of the Western World* (Chicago: Britannica, 1952), 18:625.

3This is, of course, the major theme of Genesis 3—11.

4Pattison, *The Triumph of Vulgarity*; see especially chapters 1 and 2.

5Samyutta-Nikaya, V, 420, as cited in Bhikshu Sangharakshita, *A Survey of Buddhism* (Boulder, Colo.: Shambhala, 1980), p. 114.

6*On Christian Doctrine* I. 3.

7Johannes Kepler, *Harmonies of the World*, trans. C. G. Wallis, in *Great Books of the Western World* (Chicago: Britannica, 1952), 16:1080.

8Cited by C. G. Wallis, "Translator's Introduction," *Great Books of the Western World*, 16:487.

9Annie Dillard, *Pilgrim at Tinker Creek* (New York: Bantam Books, 1974), p. 51.

10The entire passage (Mt 10:26-39) deals with the subject of fear and the loss (or finding) of one's self.

11Cf. 1 Corinthians 13.

12*Paradise*, XXXI.30.

Chapter 11: Recovering the Hope of Heaven

1V. I. Lenin, *Selected Works in Three Volumes* (Moscow: Progress Publishers, 1975), p. 715.

2Vaclav Havel, "Havel on Hope," *New Perspectives Quarterly* 8, no. 2 (Spring 1991):49.

3Arnold Toynbee suggested this in an essay, "Christianity and Civilization," when he wrote, "The Christian Church itself rose out of the spiritual travail which was a consequence of the breakdown of the Greco-Roman civilization." And about the vital insight that Christianity provided for these times, he wrote: "If religion is a chariot, it looks as if the wheels on which it mounts towards Heaven may be the periodic downfall of civilizations on Earth." *Civilization on Trial*

(New York: Oxford University Press, 1948), pp. 235-36.

[4]Some of the more important works on this topic include Karl Löwith, *Meaning in History* (1949); Norman Cohn, *The Pursuit of the Millennium* (1961); Eric Voegelin's essay "Ersatz Religion" in *Science, Politics and Gnosticism* (1968); Gerhart Niemeyer, *Between Nothingness and Paradise* (1971); and more recently Christopher Lasch, *The True and Only Heaven* (1991). Hans Blumenberg argues against this thesis in his 1966 book *The Legitimacy of the Modern Age*. The unsatisfactory elements in his argument (concisely revealed by Lasch) only help confirm the idea that modern faith in progress owes its existence to the motive force of a Christian and Jewish concept of history as a pilgrimage toward a messianic age.

[5]Christopher Lasch, *The True and Only Heaven: Progress and Its Critics* (New York: Norton, 1991), p. 39.

[6]I have attempted to deal more fully with the implications of the demise of communist governments in "Communism's Collapse: The Receding Shadow of Transcendence," *The Christian Century*, 2 May 1990.

[7]Lance Morrow, "Evil," *Time*, 10 June 1991, p. 51.

[8]Albert Camus, "Helen's Exile," in *The Myth of Sisyphus and Other Essays*, trans. Justin O'Brien (New York: Vintage Books, 1955), p. 135.

[9]Ibid., p. 136.

[10]Lasch, *True and Only Heaven*, p. 16.

[11]Ibid., p. 17.

Appendix: Philosophies of Temporal Happiness

[1]Richard Weaver, *Ideas Have Consequences* (Chicago: University of Chicago Press, 1948), pp. 2-3.

[2]Ibid., pp. 3-4.

[3]Jürgen Moltmann, *God in Creation* (San Francisco, Harper & Row, 1985), p. 30. Genesis 2:15, Moltmann points out, "talks about 'the Garden of Eden' which human beings are 'to till and keep.' So human mastery over the earth is intended to resemble the cultivating and protective work of a gardener. Nothing is said about predatory exploitation."

[4]Ibid., p. 27.

[5]R. Descartes, *Discours de la méthode* (1692), cited by Moltmann, *God in Creation*, p. 27.

[6]In a book on rock music, *The Triumph of Vulgarity*, Pattison points out that the popular expression of pantheism becomes a preference for vulgarity, i.e. things that are common and unrefined by attention to forms, convention, morals and manners.

[7]C. J. Kraus pointed this out when he commented on the ubiquity of pantheism: "Pantheism confirms itself as an authentic natural product of the human mind by the fact that it has arisen on the Ganges as on the Rhine, and in the age of Xenophanes as in that of Spinoza, and among Brahmins, Cabalists and mystics, theologians and philosophers—in short, everywhere and always, and in all kinds of intellects" ("Uber den Pantheismus," in *Vermischte Schriften*, vol. 12). Like the other two developments I mentioned, pantheism does not necessarily spread outward from some philosophy or religion so much as it represents a central tendency in the human heart and mind that is so universal that its expression is inevitably found from time to time, and necessarily feeds that hunger for asserting the self-will over the environment.

[8]Cited in G. S. Kirk and J. E. Raven, *The Presocratic Philosophies* (Cambridge, U.K.: Cambridge University Press, 1971), p. 191.

[9]Ibid., 192.